POSTMODERNISM, UNRAVELING RACISM, AND DEMOCRATIC INSTITUTIONS

POSTMODERNISM, UNRAVELING RACISM, AND DEMOCRATIC INSTITUTIONS

John W. Murphy
and Jung Min Choi

Westport, Connecticut
London

Library of Congress Cataloging-in-Publication Data

Murphy, John W.
    Postmodernism, unraveling racism, and democratic institutions /
John W. Murphy and Jung Min Choi.
        p.   cm.
    Includes bibliographical references and index.
    ISBN: 0–275–95664–4 (alk. paper)
    1. Race relations. 2. Racism. 3. Democracy. 4. Postmodernism—
Social aspects. I. Choi, Jung Min. II. Title.
HT1521.M83   1997
305.8—dc21   97–5589

British Library Cataloguing in Publication Data is available.

Library of Congress Catalog Card Number: 97–5589
ISBN: 0–275–95664–4

First published in 1997

Praeger Publishers, 88 Post Road West, Westport, CT 06881
An imprint of Greenwood Publishing Group, Inc.

Printed in the United States of America

The paper used in this book complies with the
Permanent Paper Standard issued by the National
Information Standards Organization (Z39.48–1984).

10 9 8 7 6 5 4 3 2 1

Contents

What Makes This Work Postmodern?

Given the title of this book, the following is a reasonable question: What makes this work postmodern? After all, the term postmodern appears in a myriad of book titles nowadays. In many cases, calling a book postmodern seems to be a public relations ploy to increase a book's sales. To be sure, a significant amount of controversy surrounds the use of this term.

Nonetheless, a reader is often left wondering about the thrust of postmodernism. Indeed, this idea is seldom clearly defined. Accordingly, a postmodern work might be associated with stylistic innovations; or, and more regularly, a book is touted to be postmodern if terms such as difference, fragmentation, and discourse are prominent. Although these ideas are significant, their appearance does not necessarily make a book postmodern.

Difference may simply be a novel substitute for exotic, while fragmentation may be associated with disorder or chaos. Postmodernism, however, is not this facile. To properly understand terms such as these, the philosophical gambit made by postmodernists must be grasped. When the anti-dualistic demarche advanced by postmodernists is appreciated, postmodern terminology acquires meaning that is regularly obscured. Accordingly, this work is postmodern because metanarratives are acknowledged to be incredulous. In fact, this theme goes to the core of Lyotard's definition of postmodernism.[1]

A metanarrative is an idea that has been used to sustain knowledge or order, but is not implicated respectively in the process of discovery or the activities of everyday life. For example, God, the state, the market, and functional imperatives have been adopted to underpin society. When applied to race relations, evolutionary imperatives, physical and genetic properties, and cultural mandates have served a similar purpose. Specifically, these themes have been employed to guide race relations policies, which have been concerned mostly with the issue of integration. In other words, the key task has been enforcing assimilation, and thus engendering a common culture. But because of the presence of metanarratives, integration has resulted mostly in race domination.

Because these metanarratives are assumed to be universal, groups that most exemplify these ideals have had enormous power. They have been able, in short, to demand the subordination of those who are unfortunate enough to not have these traits. Therefore, race domination is justified by principles to which everyone is supposed to adhere. Traditionally, from the pre-Socratics to the present, ideals have been accorded this power.

THE IN-BETWEEN

Deprived of recourse to metanarratives, knowledge and order must emerge from quotidian concerns. Specifically, metanarratives are rendered passé by linguistic *praxis*. Because there is no escape from language use, and thus interpretation, dualism is undermined along with the usual location of metanarratives. As Richard Rorty notes, scouring the usual places for an ahistorical foundation to ground reality is futile.[2] Now everything that is known must be viewed to be a product of interpretation, even so-called universals. Postmodernists are antimetaphysical in this regard.

As Martin Buber describes this process, everything resides in the realm of the "in-between."[3] Nothing that happens to persons occurs or is caused by something outside of this arena. This is the domain of experience that links persons—the sphere of intersubjectivity. As a result, there are no hidden forces to justify, for example, identity or institutions. Accordingly, using genes to explain intellectual inferiority is no longer simply a matter of physiology. Questions must now be raised pertaining to how and why credence has been given to genetics and who may benefit from the inferiorization of a particular group. If institutions are an outgrowth of interaction between persons, science is no exception. Furthermore, inferiorization must also be the result of this discourse. Certain persons are simply successful in stigmatizing the cultural or physical traits of others. Invoking science to legitimize this outcome only obscures the exercise of power that has occurred.

METAPHYSICS OF DOMINATION

Postmodernists do not necessarily focus on the material aspects of discrimination. Marxists, for example, have done an admirable job in illustrating the class dynamics of racism. Clearly, profit is made from all forms of discrimination. But emphasizing the material side of racism has had a paradoxical effect. Simply put, social stratification has tended to be reified; race relations are understood to be regulated by economic laws. In the end, improved race relations are thought to result from altering the economic conditions of a society. Yet changes in race relations do not seem to follow this kind of causal sequence.

Postmodernists argue that race relations will not improve appreciably until the metaphysics of racism is challenged and exposed to be illegitimate. Because of the ubiquity of language, this metaphysics is symbolic. A specific human trait or composite of traits is elevated in a manner similar to a Platonic Form.[4] Given this exalted status, these characteristics are provided the latitude to overshadow all others. In this way, the standards of assimilation come to be viewed as seignorial, and, likewise, the process of marginalization appears to be rational. But deprived of this metanarrative, assimilation and inferiorization must be predicated on *doxa*, in this case a linguistic formation, which is traditionally thought to be insufficient for this task. Opinion, in short, is not significant enough to support domination; a more profound rationale is necessary to justify this endeavor.

This call for an attack on the metaphysics of racism may sound similar to Gunnar Myrdal's argument that racism in America is mostly a moral dilemma. Eliminating the conflict between the ideal and the reality of the so-called American creed will somehow eliminate racism. But as many of Myrdal's critics declared, racism is not something that operates merely in the minds or hearts of people, but is a myriad of practices that are designed to subjugate a large segment of the population.

Talking about the need to undermine the metaphysics of racism is not intended to draw attention away from these discriminatory activities. To emphasize the point, racism consists of unscrupulous behavior and not simply abstract quandaries to be debated by philosophers. Nonetheless, specific philosophical principles have been pressed into service by supremacists to justify racist behavior. Racism will not be uprooted completely, therefore, until this dimension of discrimination is addressed.

The aim of postmodernism is not merely to eliminate barriers to integration, although this aim is certainly worthy. What postmodernists feel has not been addressed is the entire justification for integration. What is the culture of racism, which is predicated on a unique metaphysics?[5] In other words, why should certain traits be accepted as inherently universal? Once ideals are revealed to be contested interpretations, postmodernists argue that an open society, based on real pluralism, can be established.

CULTURE IS CULTURAL

As is well documented, postmodernists are committed to multiculturalism. They believe that assimilation is reductionistic and, in the end, very damaging to American society. But the path toward multiculturalism has been blocked, they argue, by a variant of the traditional foundationalist position. Foundationalism encompasses a wide range of metanarratives designed to provide culture with an indubitable base.[6]

Some cultures have claimed to be directly linked to this ultimate foundation. As a result, reminiscent of Matthew Arnold, select cultures are thought to embody human ideals while others are not. Some cultures transcend time and are more profound than those that represent particular interests. These special cultures are ahistorical and should be emulated by everyone.

In a manner of speaking, these true cultures are not cultural; they do not share any of the flaws associated with less developed societies. Indeed, making comparisons between Western civilization and societies with underdeveloped cultures has been quite common. Nowadays, the so-called "ghetto culture" is compared to white society. The aim of these comparisons, of course, is to illustrate the categorical separation between superior and inferior cultures. With regard to historical development, a complete break is present between these two domains.

Postmodernists demonstrate the untenability of this argument by showing that all cultures are contingent; all cultures serve a particular purpose and reflect specific values. All cultures, in short, are cultural, and elevating one above all others is a symbolic and political activity. No longer are comparisons legitimate that contrast civilization to faux cultures. Instead, various cultures must vie for recognition.

Hence, moving toward a multicultural society does not automatically represent a perversion of history, contrary to what critics of multiculturalism claim. A choice is not being made to embrace barbarism at the expense of reason and progress. What multiculturalists desire is to open society so that a wide range of cultural options can be recognized. In other words, cultures that have been obscured or repressed by supremacist claims will be allowed to come to fruition unimpeded. An "unguided" or free discussion will be encouraged about cultural options.[7] In this sense, all postmodernists encourage is a vibrant pluralism.

PROLIFERATION OF DIFFERENCE

The recognition of difference is also very important to postmodernists, but difference does not refer to oddities or pariahs. Difference is not something abnormal. In fact, all of these designations presuppose the metanarrative of normalcy that postmodernists question. Given this narrative, however, black is simply different from white; women are the opposite of men. In view of this juxtaposition, a negative value is attached to difference. Difference is the absence of what is anticipated.

When conceived in this way, difference should not be expected to expand, because difference is antagonistic to the normative core of society. Consistent with their view of metanarratives, postmodernists maintain that norms do not exist *sui generis*; norms are not the antipode of difference. To be specific, norms are instituted through language and are reinforced through a variety of symbols, and because of this linguistic origin, norms represent a mode of difference that has come to be accepted as natural. Accordingly, the status of a reality *sui generis* associated traditionally with norms is a fabrication. "The concept of difference has nothing ontological about it," writes Wittig, "It is only the way the masters interpret a historical situation of domination."[8] Likewise, norms are tied to nothing but human will; they "float," as postmodernists say, untied to any foundational anchor.

Because of this change in thinking about norms, the proliferation of difference is not antagonistic to normativeness. Traditional norms are nothing but difference; innovations, likewise, are simply another version of norms. Any attempt to stifle difference, therefore, must be undertaken in the name of difference. The asymmetry that usually exists between so-called progressive and backward cultures is thus exposed to be a contrivance.[9] For example, Europeans can claim to be at the center of human development, but this location is no longer secure. Because societies are comprised of nothing but cultural differences, they can be combined into any number of configurations. Europeans can be deprived of prominence without jeopardizing progress, order, or civilization.

Rather than focusing on the aberrational, postmodernists want to avoid reifying culture by emphasizing difference. Accordingly, difference signals a contest over norms and the idea that societies do not have to be culturally monolithic for them to survive. Difference represents a call for inclusion without assimilation. Persons or groups can be accepted on their own terms as different, and not have to fear marginalization. As opposed to cultural chauvinism, difference relates to a reciprocity of perspectives and tolerance for alternative norms. In this regard, Iris Young's phrase, "heterogeneous public," describes the polity postmodernists have in mind.[10]

ORDER AND THE OTHER

Treating difference as peripheral to society is manifested as disregard for the Other. Similar to culture, order has traditionally been conceived in a metaphysical manner. The metanarrative pertaining to an Archimedean point of order has been the centerpiece of modern sociology. Social ontological realism is the phrase that has been used to classify this approach to conceptualizing order.[11] Realists argue that order reflects a reality—norms, laws, or cultural mandates—that is immune to the ambiguity of daily existence.

Social morality is built on the inculcation of these universal standards. What role could the Other possibly play in this scenario? Recognizing and understanding the Other, treating the Other as truly alter, is not required for order to prevail. Actually, consulting the Other, who has a local and indeterminate existence, may obscure the rules that hold society together. Recognizing and responding sensitively to the Other may detract attention away from the cultural universals that allegedly sustain order. Emotion may taint the standards that impart morality, thereby encouraging persons to act irresponsibly.

In the absence of this metanarrative of order, postmodernists claim that the Other is indispensable for securing societal concord. Unable to invoke absolutes to join persons or groups, engaging the Other is mandatory for insuring the survival of order. A "carnal ethic," writes Luce Irigaray, becomes essential for preserving society.[12] At the level of intersubjectivity, the self and the Other are united in the flesh through an intermingling of touch, sight, and other corporeal means. Differences are thus joined without the presence of the universals that tend to become the adversary of minorities. How can a universal be anything but antagonistic to the status of a minority?

Rather than peripheral to society, the Other is integral to maintaining order. Since all persons are Others, their mutual recognition is the thread that holds society together. Thus, society is without a core; a constellation of Others constitutes order. This imagery may seem fragmented to a realist, but to a postmodernist order without a metanarrative is very coherent.[13] All that is missing are the universals that demand the subservience of the Other.

DISORDER IS NOT CHAOS

Traditionalists in the field of race relations also support the metanarrative of order. They assume that a specific arrangement of social factors represent order, while deviations from this pattern are chaotic. Challenges to assimilation, and the need for a common culture presupposed by this principle, are thought to be potentially anomic. As with all metanarratives, order is given a special identity.

To sustain this position, a complete break is presumed to exist between order and disorder. Order and disorder do not simply represent rival modes of organization. If this were the case, order would not be so valuable. Disorder, instead, consists of a complete absence of logic or regularity—unqualified unpredictability. Considering this situation, no wonder attacks on the status quo are feared, for the collapse of order is unthinkable. Presumably, abandoning assimilation would simply be the end of culture.

The problem with this portrayal is that disorder is incomprehensible. How would disorder even be known or experienced unless this arrangement could be recognized? Accordingly, positing the complete absence of a pattern or organization requires that disorder be treated as ethereal. Conversely, order becomes a cultural icon, the epitome of reason.

Here again, dualism is witnessed. Without assigning order and disorder to different planes, a clear differentiation between these two phenomena could not be maintained. Order and disorder would have to be viewed merely as different modes of organization. An alternative perspective may look chaotic, but a total absence of order is impossible. In terms of postmodern theory, disorder is a relative notion.

What is the relevance of this claim for race relations? As noted, postmodernists are known to be advocates of multiculturalism. Critics fear, however, that this process will culminate in anarchy. Presenting competing perspectives on history or the quality of literature is thought to invite the demise of civilization. But disorder is not this obvious; disorder is a matter of perspective and interest. Disorder, in other words, is an approach to order that is unacceptable or unforeseen. When viewed in this manner, expanding society is not so scary. A true pluralism does not have to be anathema to civility. Rather, disorder is merely a version of order that can be embraced or rejected. No ultimate claims are shattered or affirmed, moreover, by this choice.

CONCLUSION: WORKING WITHOUT A SAFETY NET

This work is postmodern because an analysis of race is undertaken from within the "in-between." No metaphysical props are introduced to justify identity, institutions, or social change. Discrimination, for example, is not described to be the product of social forces, economic or otherwise, but is illustrated to be the outcome of a battle between discursive formations. Racism, accordingly, is a symbolic activity that has many dimensions, some of which involve physical force and other styles of coercion. These coercive measures, nonetheless, have a symbolic core that is powerful but should not be equated with a material facade.

Nevertheless, this conclusion does not imply that postmodernists eschew so-called macroanalysis. Certainly racism is a group or collective phenomenon involving institutional barriers and the exercise of power. Behind all these claims about structures, however, are attempts to legitimize a particular discourse about race, which includes supremacist ideas. Assimilation, for instance, is based on culturally established ideals, rather than universal norms and principles. And appeals to evolution represent a strategy to reinforce race domination.

Reminiscent of Marx, postmodernists do not merely strive to describe the world. For example, identifying the variables that support racial discrimination is not an adequate form of analysis. Knowing that economic advantage is secured by racism does not go far enough. For postmodernists, the type of archaeology undertaken by Foucault is more important.[14] In this kind of study, researchers are concerned with the interpretive framework that distinguishes fact from opinion, the social processes that elevated this scheme to prominence, the socially thematic association between variables, and how personal or group relationships are altered by these linkages. Subsequent to taking this approach, insight can be gained into how social existence is created and problems are manufactured, and the impact of these activities on the formation of classes and ethnic groups can be understood.

For example, why should race be explained by a science such as biology? Furthermore, what rhetoric has been used to convince the public that such an explanation makes sense? How have persons been persuaded that science has this power? And what social dynamic—power or more subtle coercion—has been involved in giving primacy to science and identifying certain racial traits to be inferior? As a result of asking these questions, racism is not simply examined, but the racialization of interaction is explored.

In relation to employment, for example, blacks and whites exhibit very similar behavior. Both groups are selective in the jobs they desire, will not work if a wage is too low, and will always be looking for higher pay that requires less work. But when blacks describe these features of their job search they are viewed to be lazy, while whites are considered to be shrewd. How did this race-based discrepancy come to be accepted as normal? Furthermore, who would most likely benefit from having race linked to job performance and wage rates? Postmodernists labor in the in-between to discover the discursive practices that answer these and other questions related to discrimination and the prospects for creating a multicultural society.

NOTES

1. Jean-François Lyotard, *The Postmodern Condition* (Minneapolis: University of Minnesota Press, 1984), xxiv.

2. Richard Rorty, *Philosophy and the Mirror of Nature* (Princeton, N.J.: Princeton University Press, 1979).

3. Martin Buber, *Between Man and Man* (New York: Macmillan, 1978), 203.

4. Étienne Balibar, *Masses, Classes, Ideas* (New York: Routledge, 1994), 191–204.

5. David Theo Goldberg, *Racist Culture* (Oxford: Blackwell, 1993).

6. Stanley Fish, *Doing What Comes Naturally* (Durham, N.C.: Duke University Press, 1989), 344–345.

7. Paul Feyerabend, *Science in a Free Society* (London: NLB, 1978), 29–30.

8. Monique Wittig, *The Straight Mind and Other Essays* (Boston: Beacon Press, 1992), 29.

9. Colette Guillaumin, *Racism, Sexism, Power, and Ideology* (London: Routledge, 1995), 67–73.

10. Iris Marion Young, "Polity and Group Difference: A Critique of the Idea of Universal Citizenship," *Ethics* 99, no. 2 (1989): 258.

11. Werner Stark, *The Fundamental Forms of Social Thought* (New York: Fordham University Press, 1963), 1–13.

12. Luce Irigaray, *An Ethics of Sexual Difference* (Ithaca, N.Y.: Cornell University Press, 1993), 17.

13. Walter Benjamin, *Reflections* (New York: Harcourt Brace Jovanovich, 1978), 229.

14. Michel Foucault, *The Archaeology of Knowledge* (London: Routledge, 1989).

Chapter 1

The Sociological Tradition and Race Relations

DUALISM AND WESTERN PHILOSOPHY

A prominent position has been held in the Western tradition for the belief that reliable knowledge must be severed from quotidian concerns. Everyday life is replete with values, beliefs, and commitments that must be overcome if truth is ever to be acquired. The early Greeks referred to this contaminated knowledge as *doxa*, which is nowadays translated to mean opinion. Accordingly, something more profound than this muddled information must be sought to secure accurate knowledge and lasting order. A more certain base must be established for these phenomena.

For this reason, Western philosophy has been identified as "foundationalist" in thrust. What is meant by this term is that an ahistorical ground—divorced from situational contingencies and unbiased—has been pursued in a variety of ways. As described by Stanley Fish, the aim has been to "anchor the universe and thought from a point above history and culture."[1] The discovery of this foundation is assumed to legitimize judgments about facts or morals. With such a referent, certainty can be guaranteed about the key institutions of society. Speculation and ambiguity can thus be avoided.

Central to the search for this Archimedean or absolute point is the validity of dualism. It is assumed that a complete break can be made from experience, interpretation, and other human foibles that block the search for truth. The human presence can be vacated so that an unadulterated perspective can be achieved. Further, a value-free means is assumed to be available to guide this search for security and certainty.

The pre-Socratics were interested primarily in the physical character of the universe. They strove to explain the natural harmony and order that any keen observer could not miss. What each of these writers advanced is a regulatory principle that is presumed to give nature direction and purpose. For example, Thales proposed that water is the primordial principle, while Anaximenes believed that air held this position. Later on, Number, *logos*, and *nous* were posited to be the origin of the universe.[2]

Views that might seem innocuous, and by today's standards perhaps silly, established a dangerous asymmetry between individuals and the source of wisdom. Plato's allegory of the cave is a prime example of how daily life is degraded. According to Plato, the original condition of persons is to wander among the shadows and wallow in ignorance. But escape from this condition is possible. To achieve insight, however, they must abandon their bodily presence and renounce all ties to the flesh. Plato's point is that only through pure thought and entry into the realm of Ideas can salvation be attained. Following this maneuver, nonsense is avoided and a truly rational account of events can be entertained.

Although Aristotle is thought to be more down to earth, a similar theme is witnessed in his work on logic. In his *Posterior Analytics*, he outlined the beginnings of the Law of Identity (A = A), Law of Difference (B = B), and the Law of the Excluded Middle (A ≠ B). Through the use of this symbolism, knowledge is assumed to be reduced to pristine bits of information. Indeed, contingency and uncertainty are eliminated by the charge that A ≠ B. Aristotle argues that a person cannot be an animal and other than an animal at the same time; in more modern terms, minorities are categorically distinct from the social mainstream.[3] In other words, "A" has an identity that cannot be mistaken for any other element. Later on, both Hegel and Leibniz refer to the designation of A = A as devoid of distinctions and thus absolute.[4] But clearly everyday existence is not this unambiguous.

Mysticism similar to that encouraged by Plato pervades the Medieval Period. During this time, the flesh was linked to sin, but through meditation and a variety of other mendicant practices the temptations of the flesh can be suppressed. Through this kind of training, the *naturale lumen* might be envisioned. God might be known, thereby illustrating the secondary importance of civic authority and worldly ambitions and rewards. Here again, the existence of the sacred is detached from the excesses of the body.

Around 1600, the dualism found in these earlier writers was formalized by Descartes. Similar to the other philosophers, he sought wisdom, but he rejected their metaphysics and speculation, particularly the admixture of faith and reason concocted by the church fathers. Any link to uncertainty, argued Descartes, would allow persons to be tricked. In fact, at times Descartes believed he was being hoodwinked by an "evil genius."

To calm his anxiety, as some critics have called it, Descartes made his now famous philosophical demarche. He declared that *res cogito* can and should be removed unequivocally from *res extensa*. In this case, *cogito* does not simply refer to the physical mind, but to any sort of uncorroborated thought. Faith in God and unfounded propositions about reason are products of the *cogito*. Eventually, consciousness was identified as speculative, and routine thinking became known as subjective and a source of error. As a result, reason was finally completely disembodied or attributed to a mind that has no association with the human condition.

By separating the *res cogito* and *res extensa*, Descartes established a place for uncontaminated facts to reside. He cleared a space of all the elements that tend to occlude clear and distinct knowledge. In this way, he posed the possibility of encountering truly objective evidence, because knowing is "entirely dependent on the object which affects our senses."[5] Moreover, a referent is now available to measure the veracity of any claim. The *res extensa* is isolated in such a manner that a truly universal and uniform base of judgment can be invoked.

There is little doubt that Descartes's work has been construed in various ways. What is most important at this juncture is that his differentiation of the *res cogito* and the *res extensa* has come to mean that subjectivity can be severed neatly from objectivity. More to the point, subjectivity is antithetical to objectivity, and thus anything associated with the subjective side of this dualism should be removed from the search for true knowledge.[6]

The problem with Descartes's schism relates to comprehending the actual content of the *res extensa*. How is this knowledge ever to be known, if the knower—the human factor—must be dismissed as a source of bias? Excluding subjectivity, in other words, seems to contradict the need for a knower.

Empiricists such as Hume and Locke provide an answer to this conundrum. Perhaps a knower could be envisioned to merely copy or reflect reality; perhaps the mind could be portrayed as simply recording input. If this were the case, facts could be grasped without any distortion. Further, the irrationality of a mindless knower could thus be overcome. There should be no surprise, accordingly, that Locke refers to the mind as a *tabula rasa* on which data are directly imprinted. As a blank slate, the mind does not interfere with this recording process.

Yet this is only half of the story. Input must be stripped of anything that could be considered conjectural. Anything that could be viewed as added by the mind must be removed. Hence, empiricists argue that all knowledge consists of nothing more than sense impressions. These are minute fragments of matter that impinge on the mind. In the end, inanimate data are projected onto the mind, and thus the *res extensa* is confronted and copied.

Nonetheless, associating data this closely with experience was bound to cause difficulties. Could knowledge ever be recounted in such a mechanical way? Witness Locke's confusion, for example, over the roles played by primary and secondary qualities in identifying knowledge. Apparently the mind always adds something to whatever is known. Even Hume, who is hardly an idealist, recognized that the mind must exhibit an organizational capacity if sense data are going to have any form. Dualism, therefore, appears to be difficult to maintain.

Yet modern positivists felt they had a solution to this impasse. They believed a conduit could be provided for information which would prevent the intermingling of physical and mental factors. They borrowed the early Greek notion of *techné* and gave it a modern meaning. Certain techniques, they argued, could be invented that are autonomous and dispassionate. "Technique alone is rigorously objective," writes Ellul, "It blots out all personal opinions."[7] Hence, through the use of these mechanisms the search for knowledge can be deanimated.

Instruments have been invented that are touted to be devoid of metaphysics.[8] These devices are governed by mathematics, logic, and the principle of standardization, and thereby create the illusion that unbiased research can be undertaken. In point of fact, Ackerman contends that the development of this instrumentation is responsible for scientific progress. By following step-wise instructions based on alleged universal language and practices, procedures can be implemented that do not require interpretation. The search for knowledge, therefore, does not reflect personal inclinations, but instead follows rigorous and indubitable guidelines. Knowledge is conveyed through methods that are neutral and supposedly unaffected by any mode of interpretation. The facts that are discovered are thus obdurate and obtrusive.

In general, the message that has been suggested by dualism has three parts. First, the justification for universal norms does exist, although this foundation may be temporarily occluded. Second, the human element is capricious and hopelessly flawed, and thus must be constrained or neutralized in any serious pursuit of knowledge. Third, autonomous mechanisms can be constructed to gather or represent objective information. As a result of this outlook, the belief still survives that wisdom unaffected by human shortcomings can be gained.

TRADITIONAL SOCIOLOGY

The so-called founders of sociology are known for their conservative response to the social conditions in France during the 1800s. Both Comte and Durkheim believed that French society was on the verge of *anomie*. If something was not done, a complete "spiritual breakdown" was likely to occur. Social cohesion and solidarity, in other words, would likely vanish, along with tradition and the accompanying sense of security.

What France was experiencing was the onset of capitalism. And as Raymond Aron,[9] and more recently Daniel Bell, recognized, this mode of economic exchange is accompanied by a particular cultural formation.[10] Emphasized, for example, are individualism, the pursuit of personal gain, materialism, and competition between individuals and various segments of society. As a consequence, rivalry and conflict become the norm as persons strive to survive. What Comte and Durkheim witnessed was a proliferation of social divisions which had economic motives as their cause. In this sense, writes Cornel West,

"Market morality puts money-making, buying and selling, or hedonistic self-indulgence at the center of one's behavior."[11] Clearly, the end result of this mentality is a loss of community; the social implications of individual behavior are, at best, an afterthought.

The remedies that have been proposed for this condition, throughout the history of conventional sociology, have been fundamentally dualistic. Order can be based on negotiation, debate, and consensus, thereby erecting institutions on human action. But in Cartesian terminology the *res cogito* would be at the core of such a society. Such a flimsy foundation, however, has not been considered sufficient to maintain order. Norms infected by psychology and subjectivity, Durkheim writes, would be tied to desire and unstable.[12]

Auguste Comte's solution was to have order embody a universal Public Opinion. Despite the name, this body of knowledge has nothing to do with *doxa*. In fact, Comte believes that this sort of opinion leads to nothing more than intellectual anarchy. Devoid of an absolute referent, society would devolve into a melange of competing claims. Therefore, something must rise above the din of conflicting opinions to give society direction.

Comte argued that science should supply the norms necessary for order to be preserved. He was an early advocate of positive science, and thus believed in value-freedom. Consistent with Descartes, Comte believed that fact can be severed from value. Specifically, value can be sequestered to the extent that objective facts can be revealed. Through experimentation and observation, the hallmark of positive science, facts can be accumulated into a uniform body of knowledge.

By relying on the physical sciences, Comte believed sociology could become a "social physics." Armed with rigorous methods and empirically based theory, sociologists can successfully intervene and repair any society. Science has this power because it can generate information that is ultimately factual and accessible to average citizens. Moral order, claims Comte, can best be created and preserved by those who have proper scientific credentials.[13] Others, he argues, are too enamored of freedom and personal opinion to become disciplined enough to reveal or adhere to natural laws.

In addition to his epistemology, Comte advanced a style of social imagery he believed would quell *anomie*. He declared that society should be compared to a living organism. Simply put, he is an advocate of the organismic analogy. By making this choice, Comte rejected the moral philosophies of Adam Smith, Kant, and the utilitarians. Although these theories are quite different, he believed they made a common error. Because the individual holds a prominent position in each theory, subjectivity is united too closely to morality. Comte contends, for example, that morals must be predicated on something more significant than sympathy or happiness. In addition, he believes the market will destroy French society because of the stress that is placed on individualism and personal gain. In this regard, the market cannot be trusted to transform personal ambition into collective prosperity.

On the other hand, when people are told that their society represents an organism, the idea is emphasized that the individual is subordinate to some greater whole. Moreover, like a body, the parts of the social organism are integrated and, unless disrupted, exist in a state of harmony. In a manner similar to Aristotle, Comte described society to have its own *telos*. The task of each person is to adjust to the demands of the social system so that its homeostasis is not disturbed for very long. By stressing the functional interdependence of society's components, Comte assumed persons will begin to understand that morality does not depend on the wishes of individuals. Morality, instead, has a rationale of its own; morality is not a property of personal psychology, motives, or behavior.

In true dualistic fashion, Comte, and later Spencer, de-emphasized the individual by focusing on the organismic base of morality. Nonetheless, Durkheim thought these writers did not sufficiently separate reality from imagination. After all, hardly anyone who examines society finds an organism; equating the body with society is thus a metaphor. But, as Durkheim writes, society does seem to constitute a reality that can constrain and coerce persons.[14] In an effort to describe this force, Durkheim minimally utilizes the organismic analogy because of its imaginary and thus speculative character.

Durkheim's final proposal, however, is no less abstract, despite his claims to the contrary. As practically every sociology student knows, Durkheim announced that society is synonymous with a reality *sui generis*. Giving society this seignorial status, he believed, insures social solidarity. This reality, he writes, is "irreducible . . . to the psychic nature of the individual," and more powerful than all individuals combined.[15] Hence, society has the stature required to enlist support from all of its members. Obligation does not stem from a sense of personal duty, but is derived from societal imperatives. A priori strictures are presumed to exist that impose morality.

While imaginary bodies are not involved, Durkheim's thesis is clearly abstract. Nonetheless, he maintains that this level of abstraction is necessary to preserve order from corrupt human influences. He illustrates that a reality *sui generis* is more reliable than the government, the state, or any other political artifice. These other entities may be manipulated to reflect particular interests, as expressed by a cabal of investors or conspirators, while this exalted reality is immune to such intrigue. This reality *sui generis* exemplifies what Descartes had in mind by *res extensa*.

The social, therefore, is able to instill moral constraint. This outcome is possible, Durkheim claims, because the "social always possesses a higher dignity than what is individual."[16] Accordingly, this reality *sui generis* is impersonal, exact, objective, and, as Durkheim likes to say, necessitating. Confusion is thus averted, due to the "collective consciousness" engendered by this reality. An inscrutable moral authority is present to hold society together. A force is available that is able to bend the will of persons without any of the bias that is associated with repression. For this reason, compliance with social norms is not considered to be restrictive, but virtuous.

This trend culminated in functionalism, particularly the rendition of society provided by Talcott Parsons. He admits his work is devoted to solving what he called the Hobbesian problem—the fear that society could erupt at any moment into the "war of all against all." But he did not appreciate the tact taken by Hobbes, or earlier sociologists, to address this issue. They were simply unscientific in their approach to this problem, in that myth and imagination were allowed to obscure reason.

In view of the success of cybernetics, particularly Norbert Wiener's early book on this topic, Parsons referred to society as a system. Most important, social life is described to be a system of roles—nodes of behavioral expectations—that are structurally linked. In other words, because of the principle of "double contingency," roles are bound together by a mechanism their inhabitants do not control.[17] So when Parsons talks about volition this activity is conditioned by circumstances that are presumed to have an a priori existence. Choices exist within the context of the demands imparted by roles.

Structural metaphors have become quite popular for describing the unity of roles. For example, roles have been understood as organized into sets, nets, or networks. Suggested by this terminology is that the alignment of roles does not depend on persons recognizing, liking, or agreeing with one another. Roles are united on the basis of structure and function, rather than something as unpredictable as volition. Structures, stated simply, are objective and substantial enough to forestall the onset of chaos. To be specific, structures are not influenced by interpretation and other modes of uncertainty that can cause behavior to go awry.

Parsons's use of systems theory represents a modern variant of dualism, but neither analogies nor mythical figures, such as a Leviathan, are invoked to assure interpersonal harmony. Instead, Parsons's work is an example of modern scientific thought. Roles are empirical, while they are joined by laws related to the necessary and efficient transmission of information and energy. The steering mechanisms of society, therefore, are provided with a very realistic caste.

Whereas most persons are skeptical about the presence of a social organism, they are able to relate to the idea of roles. In fact, this vocabulary has crept into everyday argot. Children are thought to need role models, while adjustment to roles is accepted almost unquestioningly as a fact of life. In this regard, Parsons's attempt to externalize the source of norms appears to be a reasonable way to preserve order.

Throughout the history of modern social thought, alternatives to this realism have emerged. Nonetheless, sociology remains overwhelmingly wedded to Cartesianism and providing norms, institutions, and other agents of order with autonomy. Although theories such as phenomenology and symbolic interactionism are quite popular in some circles, they have been referred to regularly by traditionalists as "micro-theories." The implication is that theories that elevate the human element in importance by stressing the interpretive or symbolic foundation of society are not capable of explaining social order. Society, as dualists contend, cannot be built on such an ephemeral ground.

RACE RELATIONS AND ASSIMILATION

Dualism has had an adverse effect on the field of race relations. Specifically, discussions about race have been dominated by an assimilationist perspective.[18] This finding has been true even when pluralism has been advocated. In fact, some critics have charged that the thrust of race relations in sociology has been to diminish the importance of racial and ethnic differences. Until the recent rise of multiculturalism, the focus has been on integrating everyone into society, and discovering why this end has not been achieved. Even many Marxists and other radicals have given priority to identifying and eliminating barriers to full participation in society. In the end, however, the myth of America as a glorious "melting pot," where persons from all over the globe are fused together to form a new civilization, has been preserved.[19] The existence of difference is simply a stage on the path of complete integration.

Through assimilation the racial myths of racial inferiority can be disproven. Within each minority is a human ideal, regularly linked to whiteness, which could emerge if the proper social conditions are created. The flaw in this formula, however, is that these persons must jettison their racial and cultural heritage, which is considered to be a vestigial remains. Purged of these elements, minorities can move successfully into the future. Hiding within each minority, so goes the argument, is a human being that may never be realized.

In typical dualistic fashion, an asymmetrical relationship is thought to exist between immigrants and the society they are entering. Furthermore, this source of order should not be defiled or occluded by ethnic traits and foreign traditions. Should these differences infect society, the resulting cacophony would be disastrous. Cultural relativism, as some critics contend, might gain a foothold, thereby undermining any standards of morality.[20] As a result, the structural and cultural imperatives at the heart of any prosperous society will be destroyed. Various conservative critics today contend that the West is under siege by multiculturalists. The barbarians are at the gates and they must be pushed back by a good dose of Western culture. Over time, the melting pot will work its magic. Through continual contact with the mainstream of society, immigrants will be changed and improved. Their ethnic heritage and other impurities will fade away as they become Americanized. A type of uniformity will ensue that reflects the best of humanity and society. Any rejection of this ideal is considered to be indicative of irrationality and a commitment to an archaic and inferior culture. It is assumed that reason will eventually prevail and integration will be embraced by everyone.

From the 1920s until the 1950s, the so-called Chicago School, originally headed by Robert Park and Ernest Burgess, practically monopolized discussions about race. Their famous cycle of race relations, for instance, was used as a blueprint for bussing and other integration policies in the United States. Through increasing contact with bona fide Americans, immigrants will acquire the social and job skills, education, and character essential for them to become fully assimilated. This adjustment is a natural process, implicitly tied to evolution, that will culminate in the disappearance of ghetto enclaves. At one juncture, Park remarked that assimilation is equivalent to Americanization, and that this activity is "progressive and irreversible."[21] Unless immigrants are too damaged or resistant, assimilation will follow an inevitable course. If they are too severely stigmatized—either in character or appearance—assimilation may take a very long time or may not occur at all.[22]

Even during this period of American history, not everyone agreed with Park and Burgess. These self-proclaimed pluralists, such as Horace Kallen, Randolph Bourne, and later, Nathan Glazer, Daniel P. Moynihan, and Pierre van den Berghe, argued that complete assimilation is not required for the moral base of society to survive. They argued that America might even be enriched and vitalized by cultivating cultural diversity.

Nonetheless, these pluralists never really rejected assimilation. In this regard, Omi and Winant contend that both pluralists and assimilationists recognize the "presence of a supposedly unitary majority culture."[23] Because of the influence of William James, Kallen believed that an abstract social force bound persons together. Accordingly, Kallen introduced his well-known metaphor of everyone playing a part in a similar orchestra.[24] Bourne, also affected by James, viewed society to be held together in an almost cosmic manner; and in the case of Glazer, Moynihan, and van den Berghe, naturalistic tendencies, some of which are overtly or crudely biological, are thought to be at the root of society.

Because each of these writers externalize the cause of normativeness, cultural differences are expected to be absorbed into the prevailing social system. For example, Kallen presupposed that gradually everyone would be playing similar music. Yet he did not consider this denouement to require assimilation. Perhaps this confusion stems from the fact that he deals only with European immigrants and assumes they share a single tradition. No assimilation is involved, in other words, when persons adapt to a universal heritage they have either forgotten or never learned. After giving credence to this unifying background, cooperation is possible without assimilation.

In the 1960s, in the midst of civil rights unrest, Glazer and Moynihan identified minority groups as having impaired intellectual and cultural traits, in addition to family values, that prevent them from having social mobility. The failure to develop strong family ties, save, and take advantage of educational opportunities, as well as a lack of initiative, are the characteristics that are often cited.[25] Abandoning these qualities, and recognizing the validity of the opportunity structure that is available to everyone, is key to success. What is needed is a creative response to the social system which will enable blacks and other minorities to find a niche in the economy where they can flourish. There is something wrong with the way in which minorities view American society, which may have a cognitive or a cultural origin. In any case, becoming absorbed into the economic system completely is a prerequisite for success and acceptance.

At this juncture, a brief interlude is necessary. Because pluralists never broke completely with the assimilationist outlook, pluralism is rejected by contemporary multiculturalists. The conditions are still present in pluralism, argue multiculturalists, that support race domination. Equally profound as the structural and economic issues raised by Marxists is a philosophy, referred to as the metaphysics of domination, that must be refuted if true pluralism is ever to be achieved. Because they overlook this element, pluralists require assimilation for the success of minorities; conformity to the dominant society is required for experiencing the good life. Pluralism is thus a transitory condition.

Following this brief flirtation with pluralism, although a somewhat truncated version, the focus returned to overt assimilation in a variety of forms. During the mid-1960s, Milton Gordon's views received significant attention. He recommends several areas of assimilation, including social, economic, and, indirectly, biological dimensions, with the intent of illustrating how "Anglo-conformity" can be fostered.[26] Throughout the 1970s, 1980s, and 1990s, the eugenic theories of Arthur Jensen, William Shockley, and J. Phillipe Rushton were given a public forum, along with the cultural inferiority theories resurrected by Edward Banfield and William Julius Wilson in the 1980s.[27] This trend reached a high point with the publication of Murray and Herrnstein's book, *The Bell Curve*, which supposedly represents the most scientific treatment to date of the factors related to successful assimilation.[28]

Most often these biological and bio-cultural explanations support the charge that ethnic minorities can never achieve real parity with whites. Still, a naturalistic, and thus ahistorical, rationale is introduced to support a dominant culture that all persons should at least strive to emulate. Contrary to most early American assimilationists, these new advocates of biologism are not vague about the justification for the ideals that everyone is asked to affirm. The norms guiding these approaches to assimilation are rooted, as Fanon describes accurately, in epidural conditions and derivative moral traits: "blackness, darkness, shadow, shades, night, the labyrinths of the earth, abysmal depths, blacken someone's reputation."[29] In this sense, minorities, especially non-whites, exist *sui generis*; their mental and moral corruption are thus inevitable.

This new breed of eugenicists are especially virulent. Earlier eugenic positions, which appeared throughout the history of American race relations, were based mostly on speculation. References were made, for example, to evolutionism and social Darwinism to justify discrimination. More recent styles of biological-based racism are tied to scientific proofs of inferiority. Although such findings have never been produced and will never be forthcoming, because demonstrating inferiority is not within the purview of science but is a social determination, linking racism and science in this way has fortified the racist position.

THE METAPHYSICS OF DOMINATION

As part of his discussion of anti-Semitism, Sartre argues that a metaphysical reason is necessary to demand assimilation.[30] Simply put, requiring that persons reject their heritage is very serious and cannot be predicated on whims or the vagaries of history. The ideals that persons are expected to internalize, which often demands cultural self-denial and bodily alterations, must have a privileged status. These norms must be elevated to such an extent that they do not appear to reflect particular biases, as is exemplified by political or class interests.

Such self-serving motives would hardly find widespread appeal. In other words, overt hegemony would likely be rejected, especially in a democracy, if this domination were not for the common good. Nonetheless, assimilation does represent a kind of cultural imperialism, for one set of values, beliefs, and behaviors is presumed to be superior to all others. Key to the success of assimilationist rhetoric, however, is making these ideals appear universal and their acceptance rational, uncontroversial, and beneficial to a society as a whole. In this way, cultural suppression can be viewed to be in the service of a more noble principle than personal gain; everyone benefits from assimilation, because a potential source of social conflict is eliminated. Assimilation produces the cultural universals that are supposedly necessary for the smooth operation of society.

Most important at this juncture is that dualism is at the core of establishing the cultural supremacy required for assimilation to make sense. As a result of categorically differentiating interpretation from true knowledge, the opportunity is available to assert that specific norms are fundamentally different from others. They are more pure, advanced, and indicative of modern civilization. Because of their unadulterated position, these norms are superior to the rest and truly embody the best of humanity. As Balibar describes, they illustrate unequivocally the "difference between humanity and animality."[31]

Because of this theoretical maneuver, the arbitrariness usually associated with suppression is eliminated. The necessity of adopting these norms is not debatable, except by miscreants, because these ideals are understood to be coveted by every society. Therefore, enforcing adherence to them is not an infringement on freedom but a beneficial act. Everyone wins when these cultural mores are generally accepted; society takes a step forward along the evolutionary path.

What this metaphysic encourages is the development of a clearing in which the absolutes that become cultural universals can reside. Beyond the reach of interpretation, these norms can be enforced with certainty; these standards can be imposed with impunity because of their stature. After all, these ideals are not limited by context, belief, or any other social considerations.

Emmanuel Levinas declares that this metaphysic is violent.[32] Everything historical can be rendered irrelevant and crushed beneath these absolutes. Persons can be denigrated, along with entire cultural traditions. Anything that is inconsistent with these ideals can be relegated to obscurity. Derrida agrees with Levinas's assessment that the resulting totalization of existence, supported by this search for absolutes, is imperious and very dangerous.[33] Eventually, suppression of some individuals or groups will be required for truth, culture, or order to survive. To be sure, any deviation from the norms presupposed by these phenomena must be stifled. In all cases, the universal dominates the particular, with no hope of reconciling these two elements. As a result, social life is either going to be homongeneous or repressive.

Postmodernists refer to these vaunted positions as "metanarratives."[34] They argue that these justifications constitute discursive practices, and thus are not a priori universal, and are a part of particular symbolic traditions.[35] Stated differently, these ideals reflect someone's interests, although they may be concealed behind claims about science, objectivity, and universality.[36] By rejecting metanarratives, postmodernists attempt to break the grip of a style of formalism that is regularly used to inferiorize and marginalize various segments of society.

Given this assault on dualism by postmodernists, their approach to race relations departs dramatically from the assimilationist tradition. What postmodernists advocate, broadly speaking, is multiculturalism and the accompanying open society. They note that resistance to expanding difference is organized in terms of a particular approach to codifying existence, rather than simply the result of inertia that is inherent to a hegemonic reality. Racism, in other words, is perpetuated by far more than biological laws and the existence of power differentials, for these considerations need cultural, philosophical, and other modes of support. Key facets of the race relations tradition are rethought by postmodernists, and this topic is given a new direction. For this reason, postmodernism is perceived by many mainstream social scientists to pose a threat to culture and social order. Indeed, postmodernists are not merely searching for less offensive approaches to assimilation and social integration.

Traditional sociology, specifically the trend inaugurated by Comte and Durkheim, has adopted a conservative viewpoint on knowledge and order. This perspective is especially evident in the emphasis that has been placed on assimilation in the field of race relations. A mass culture where cultural differences are restricted at best to particular pockets is made safe and stable. Postmodernists leave behind this neat and cozy description of society for one that is decidedly more daring. Interpretation is understood to go all the way down, to paraphrase Stanley Fish, thus revealing society to be an ongoing construction. With respect to understanding race and social relations, this change gives primacy to ethnic and racial difference and the need to reorganize society according to this theme. In other words, postmodernists strive to open society instead of providing a more efficient means of resolving conflicts. As opposed to even some Marxists, postmodernists want this expansion to be an ongoing process, one that does not stop with the triumph of any group. In Marxist terminology, the dialectic of difference never reaches an end.

NOTES

1. Stanley Fish, *Doing What Comes Naturally* (Durham, N.C.: Duke University Press, 1989), 30.

2. Irving M. Zeitlin, *Plato's Vision* (Englewood Cliffs, N.J.: Prentice-Hall, 1993), 31–35.

3. Frantz Fanon, *The Wretched of the Earth* (New York: Grove Weidenfield, 1991), 38–39.

4. Emmanuel Levinas, "Ethics as First Philosophy," in *Levinas Reader*, ed. Sean Hand (London: Basil Blackwell, 1989), 86–87.

5. René Descartes, "Rules for the Direction of the Mind," in *Philosophic Problems*, ed. Maurice Mandelbaum, Francis Gramlich, and Alan Ross (New York: Macmillan, 1957), 125.

6. Samuel Enoch Stumpf, *Socrates to Sartre* (New York: McGraw-Hill, 1966), 254–255.

7. Jacques Ellul, *The Technological Society* (New York: Vintage Books, 1964), 131.

8. Robert John Ackerman, *Data, Instruments, and Theory* (Princeton, N.J.: Princeton University Press, 1985), 50.

9. Raymond Aron, *Main Currents in Sociological Thought*, vol. 1 (New York: Doubleday, 1968), 83–84.

10. Daniel Bell, *The Cultural Contradictions of Capitalism* (New York: Basic Books, 1978).

11. Cornel West, *Prophetic Thought in Postmodern Times* (Monroe, Maine: Common Courage Press, 1993), 17.

12. Emile Durkheim, *Pragmatism and Sociology* (Cambridge: Cambridge University Press, 1983), 66.

13. Lewis Coser, *Masters of Sociological Thought* (New York: Harcourt, Brace, Jovanovich, 1977), 5.

14. Emile Durkheim, *Selected Writings* (Cambridge: Cambridge University Press, 1976), 64.

15. Ibid., 62.

16. Durkheim, *Pragmatism and Sociology*, 68.

17. Talcott Parsons, *The Social System* (Glencoe, Ill: Free Press, 1951).

18. Paul L. Metzger, "American Sociology and Black Assimilation: Conflicting Perspectives," *American Journal of Sociology* 76, no. 4 (1971): 627–647.

19. Israel Zangwill, *The Melting Pot* (New York: Macmillan, 1908).

20. Dinesh D'Souza, *The End of Racism* (New York: Free Press, 1995), 18–21.

21. Robert E. Park, *Race and Culture* (Glencoe, Ill.: Free Press, 1950), 151.

22. Ibid., 204–207, 208–209.

23. Michael Omi and Howard Winant, *Racial Formation in the United States* (New York: Routledge and Kegan Paul, 1986), 16.

24. Horace Kallen, *Cultural Pluralism and the American Idea* (Philadelphia: University of Pennsylvania Press, 1956), 98.

25. Nathan Glazer and Daniel P. Moynihan, *Beyond the Melting Pot* (Cambridge, Mass.: MIT Press, 1970), 33–50.

26. Milton M. Gordon, *Assimilation in American Life* (New York: Oxford University Press, 1964), 72.

27. Alan Ryan, "Review of the Bell Curve: Intelligence and Class Structure in American Life," *The New York Review of Books*, 17 November 1994, 7–11.

28. Charles Murray and Richard Herrnstein, *The Bell Curve* (New York: Free Press, 1994).

29. Frantz Fanon, *Black Skin, White Masks* (New York: Grove Weidenfeld, 1967), 189.

30. Jean-Paul Sartre, *Anti-Semite and Jew* (New York: Schocken, 1969), 40–46.

31. Étienne Balibar, "Racism and Nationalism," in *Race, Nation, Class*, ed. Étienne Balibar and Immanuel Wallerstein (London: Verso, 1991), 57.

32. Levinas, "Ethics as First Philosophy," 76–81.

33. Jacques Derrida, "Violence and Metaphysics: An Essay on the Thought of Emmanuel Levinas," in *Writing and Difference* (Chicago: University of Chicago Press, 1978), 79–153.

34. Jean-François Lyotard, *The Postmodern Condition* (Minneapolis: University of Minnesota Press, 1984), xxiv.

35. Michel Foucault, *The Archaeology of Knowledge* (London: Routledge, 1989), 31–39.

36. Stanley Fish, *Is There a Text in this Class?* (Cambridge: Harvard University Press, 1980), 257.

Chapter 2

Postmodernism:
Theoretical Considerations

REJECTION OF METANARRATIVES

Jean-François Lyotard defines postmodernism as "incredulity toward meta-narratives."[1] Throughout the Western tradition stories have been told about the origin and end of history, the ultimate source of morality, the primordial nature of good and evil, the root of knowledge, and so forth. As discussed in Chapter 1, these tales reflect the belief that the contingencies of history can be transcended. Insight is thus possible that is not clouded by the minutae of daily experience.

These grand narratives, as they are sometimes called, supply an explanation for events by locating them on a developmental itinerary. But as should be noted, this plan is not implicated in history. This guiding *telos* operates behind the scenes to insure that persons, institutions, and groups have meaning, and that their growth is unimpeded. Historical legitimation is thus achieved, writes Lyotard, through claims that have "ontological pretentions."[2]

Clearly these metanarratives are feasible because of dualism. These grand stories are pretentious precisely because they demand universal recognition; they demand a culture-free status. Without dualism and the resulting *res extensa*, these all-encompassing modes of discourse could not exist. There would be no location undefiled by assumptions and interests where they could reside. In the absence of dualism, this pure or universal knowledge would not make sense. Absolute knowledge, in short, requires a justification that is unrestricted or boundless.

As will be discussed, postmodernists demonstrate that this limitless knowledge does not exist *sui generis* or in any other form. Most important, however, is that serious problems arise when content is actually introduced into a scenario predicated on the separation of knowledge from human *praxis*. Specifically, certain positions are allotted a privileged stature that makes them especially alluring; precisely because these positions transcend contingencies, they are noteworthy. Against such a background, theories about cultural superiority are very appealing. Moreover, the desirability of particular ethnic traits can be enhanced with little difficulty. Hence, assimilation sounds like a good idea. Why would reasonable persons not want to covet these special cultural standards?

Postmodernism, however, is antagonistic to this sort of metaphysical philosophy, and accordingly undermines the metaphysics of assimilation.[3] Postmodernists reject what Jacques Derrida calls the "logocentric" tradition.[4] They refuse to identify select forms of knowledge, events, and cultures, for example, as central and others as peripheral to society. Their point is that there are no unadulterated criteria for making these and other equally damaging distinctions. There is no ultimate center around which a hierarchy of knowledge or cultures can be structured. This kind of arrangement may occur, but the typical absolutes introduced to sanction status differentials are considered to be suspect. The European center has been dislocated, writes Derrida, and thus is "forced to stop considering itself as the culture of reverence."[5] There is no place for this center to hide.

Postmodernists view dualism to be illegitimate, and therefore they believe the search for transcultural absolutes conceals political motives. Indeed, they are specifically anti-Cartesian and deny the existence of the secure base of knowledge sought by Descartes and other dualists. This does not mean that true knowledge disappears or society automatically devolves into relativism, but that societal distinctions must gain recognition through some method of interaction before they have any credibility. Objectivity is not real, in other words, simply because a mode of knowledge is attached to a dualistically based justification, one that is thought to escape the effects of interpretation. Dominant symbols do not arrive fully determined, but are socially manufactured.

All knowledge, according to postmodernists, is positional, or implicated in a range of cultural conditions. Even so-called objective information—truth, facts, and scientific evidence—derives its significance from what Michel Foucault calls an "episteme."[6] This term refers to the constellation of assumptions, or the "conditions of existence," that support a particular outlook on reality.[7] Cultural characteristics are embedded within a similar framework, thereby undercutting the universals that underpin assimilation. Isolating the so-called best of humanity and idealizing these traits is difficult when all knowledge is tainted by cultural exigencies. For this reason, Bataille laments that all knowledge is excremental or impure.[8] Metanarratives about race are therefore not as grand as they might initially seem.

Important at this juncture is that postmodernists abandon the dualism that lends credence to metanarratives. Postmodernism is not restricted to one historical period; one, presumably, that follows modernity. Many writers, therefore, who are not identified officially as postmodern advance themes that are consistent with postmodernism. Postmodern positions on knowledge and order, simply put, arise from a variety of sources. Common among all of them is a rejection of attempts to externalize and thus to absolutize social phenomena.

POSITIVISM AND GRAND DESIGNS

Postmodernists claim that dualism is passe; this philosophical maneuver, stated simply, has become extremely difficult to retain. They are critical of its many manifestations in Western philosophy, including Plato's escapism, Medieval apologists for God, and the rarefied versions of society proffered by traditional sociologists. Yet most of their attention is directed to exposing, and thus subverting, the metanarrative of positive science. In a manner similar to the Frankfurt style of critical theory, positivism is considered by postmodernists to be another ideology.

Positivism is presented in Chapter 1 as occupying a unique place in the history of dualism. For positivists, the road to pristine knowledge is unrelated to faith or any claims unrelated to the empirical world. In fact, positivism is held in high esteem because only publicly verifiable data are treated as valid. Further, non-empirical experiences are dismissed as esoteric and unimportant. Because only empirically corroborated factors are given credence, positivism is thought to make a significant advance in the pursuit of factual knowledge.

But the theme that makes positivism desirable also makes this approach to science ideological. Positivism provides accessibility to facts through the use of a "disinterested logic of inquiry."[9] Instrumentation is introduced that is self-regulating, thereby producing what Lyotard calls a "perfectly sealed circle of facts."[10] The methods employed by positivists are standardized, consistent with one another, and operate according to a completely integrated system of logic. United in this way, these factors comprise an impregnable analytic scheme, and when implemented by a properly trained technician, errors are minimized because of the systemic nature of any inquiry. Reason uncontaminated by personal bias can thus be exercised.

As Francis Bacon relates, the methodology of positive science is purged of all idols. Ambitions, desires, and other idiosyncracies that may lead persons away from the truth are removed from scientific methods. By accepting the schism between fact and value, these methodologies can be treated as rigorous and precise. The prospect that these practices embody personal choices, values, or political biases is not given serious consideration. Positivists view their methods to be unmotivated or devoid of any orientation. Their instruments simply allow facts to be revealed without any interference. Acquiring knowledge is simply a matter of technological competence.

But at this point is where the issue of ideology becomes relevant. As Marx and Engels define this idea in their book, *The German Ideology*, an ideology functions like a *camera obscura*.[11] That is, human creations are made to appear as if they are autonomous or unrelated to individual or collective *praxis*. An ideology is able to cajole persons into believing they are ancillary to, and possibly even determined by, the objects they invent and events they plan. In the end, they are expected to adapt to the world they have made.

Science is ideological because facts are generated that persons must confront. Because science is believed to be divorced from values, the *cogito* is not thought to shape the search for knowledge; but a host of writers have argued lately that the scientific process is not this mechanical. According to Thomas Kuhn, for example, science consists of conflicting paradigms—ways of conceptualizing or "mapping" reality—and the accumulation of facts is affected by decisions that do not pertain to instrumentation, logic, or methods.[12] Therefore, the collection of facts is not simply a logistical undertaking that is punctuated by crucial experiments which provide answers to key puzzles and outline the necessary course of future research. Science, instead, is replete with competing theories, political agendas, and personalities that openly vie for dominance. Science is plagued by a sense of historicity, illustrates Derrida, that requires effort to ignore.[13]

What Kuhn is saying, along with others such as Feyerabend, is that various modes of conceptualization extend to the core of the scientific enterprise. Theory, concepts, and the anticipation of certain findings influence search strategies, data collection, and how pieces of information are summarized. As opposed to being free of values, science is a culture that includes criteria for differentiating fact from fantasy. A style of play is operative that is supposed to be unlearned through professional training.[14] In this regard, science is not dualistic, but is intertwined with many so-called subjective, or unscientific, elements.

Consistent with Kuhn's constructionistic position, Lyotard declares that "scientific knowledge constitutes a kind of discourse."[15] Rather than being objective, positive science is an outgrowth of a particular way of talking about the world. Facts, for example, are imagined to be discrete "bits" of data which are material and independent of any context. Never mind that data never conform to this description, positivists continue to argue that facts have this identity. As a discursive formation, writes Foucault, science "makes possible the appearance of objects during a given period of time."[16] Through the use of a particular linguistic scheme, the conditions are established that are compatible with scientific inquiry. Science promotes a particular definition of reality which, in turn, is reinforced by the research process.

Because of this circular activity, science does not reflect or provide a snapshot of the world. Science, instead, works within a unique epistemological "threshold" that specifies the relevance of certain questions, data, and answers.[17] Further, a shift in this boundary results in reality being reconfigured; a change in discourse resulting in the need for new explanations.

With this critique of science, postmodernists are dismissing this most recent attempt to bring foundationalism to fruition. Rather than being foundational, science merely instills a perspective on the world. Science constitutes an argument and utilizes various rhetorical devices to gain credibility, rather than a complete and untainted system. There is no unfettered, scientific gateway to truth. Therefore, science must compete for recognition with other discursive formations if scientifically generated data are going to be perceived as useful. For science has no metalanguage that will guarantee it legitimacy and a prominent role in society.[18]

FOUNDATION AND POWER

Since the time of Francis Bacon, knowledge has been equated with power. This conclusion is especially true when knowledge is sustained through foundationalism. Foucault criticizes this foundationalist thesis, along with all postmodernists.[19] These very different writers strive to illustrate the contingent predicates of such power, precisely because these issues make a position vulnerable. But this vulnerability is exactly what foundationalists hope to deny. Clearly, postmodernists and foundationalists are moving in opposite directions.

Foundationalism supports power in a unique way, because dualism enables one mode of knowledge to be elevated above all others. Due to this exalted status, this information is believed to be innocent. Adhering to this special viewpoint, moreover, is thought to epitomize rational behavior and insure that society is upgraded. After all, this knowledge is pristine and above the cultural imbroglio.

Clearly, any person or group who can claim exclusive access to this information has enormous power. Having a comprehensive picture of how society operates, unclouded by distractions, is undoubtedly an advantage. Who is going to listen to persons who are parochial and unable to grasp the general rules or mechanisms that govern societal affairs? Power grows from having information that illustrates mastery of a topic or issue.

Mastery, however, can be acquired in many ways. Through dedication a person can become very skillful and gain admiration. On the other hand, by adhering to particular standards and exhibiting certain characteristics, legitimacy can be acquired. Postmodernists are not especially interested in the first approach to securing influence, but are worried about power that has a foundational or metaphysical taint. In other words, power unrelated to personal or collective undertakings is of most concern to postmodernists.

When accessibility results from work or effort, the resulting knowledge is debatable. Limitations resulting from faulty methods, a narrow focus, poor motivation, or errors in judgment are always possible. Because of human vulnerability, particular claims are always subject to debate and revision. Power that emerges through critique and discussion is viewed by postmodernists as mature, even reasonable, and not problematic. In fact, power that is won in this way reflects social concerns, both agreement and dissent, and does not pose a threat to pluralism.

Power that is achieved through appeals to foundationalism, on the other hand, represents an insidious form of terrorism. As is suggested, this kind of terror does not result from the overt suppression of differences. Indeed, when persons are presented with demands that are legitimized by foundationalist claims, they often willingly abandon their views, identities, and cultural heritage. They are intimidated by these exalted demands to the extent that they are incapable of responding and relent to this authority. In this regard, to borrow from Derrida, many minorities have lived under the terrorism of reason; they have succumbed to science and scientific experts.[20] They have knowingly altered themselves according to the rationale prescribed by science, and have often done so without overt coercion. This discipline is not viewed as barbaric, argues Foucault, because of the ostensible reasonableness of the demands.[21]

Because foundational knowledge is value-free, and thus allegedly apolitical, persons are swayed easily by this information. Science, for example, is purged of opinion and is ultimately rational and thus transcends the biases of culture. People who consider themselves enlightened, moreover, take pride in accepting scientific reports; by acknowledging the acuity of these findings, they are demonstrating their acceptance of reason. They are being progressive and denying any link to a primitive past, and are supplying evidence of their adaptability.

Most important, however, power does not appear to emanate from a particular place and is very difficult to confront. Because foundational knowledge is universal, particular interests that may benefit from this position are concealed. Scientists are neutral, so goes the argument, and thus their findings could not intentionally be racist or politically beneficial to a specific person or class. Due to the apparent rationality of scientific procedures and instruments, particularly following the advent of the computer, people do not feel assaulted by science. Therefore, people tend to internalize readily scientific explanations without any threat or force.

Nonetheless, this sort of power can be very damaging, for, as Foucault describes, it creeps slowly into the capillaries of society. His point is that power is exercised in a manner that appears to be pervasive, natural, and normative, and thus does not represent the triumph of one group over another. All persons are simply succumbing to reason, which unfortunately sometimes culminates in requiring the racial or cultural superiority of particular persons or groups. Yet because this outcome is not ostensibly political or the product of overt aggression, domination is not thought to be present.

The example Foucault uses to describe this exercise of foundational threat is "bio-power."[22] He argues that racial discrimination has been traditionally justified in this way, without calling any attention to the conflict that exists between the ideals of democracy and racism. If particular persons can be proven to be biologically inferior, they do not have a right to equal treatment. In American race relations, this line of thinking runs from the early eugenics movement to the publication of *The Bell Curve* and *Beyond Racism*. Discriminatory treatment is only logical, given the fundamental differences between persons and groups. Nature, in short, is hierarchical. As might be expected, this story is especially convincing when it is told by scientists and other disinterested observers.

In the parlance of race relations, bio-power is an example of institutionalized racism. According to Carmichael and Hamilton, who popularized this term, racism is institutionalized when this form of discrimination is rationalized by formalized practices which, because of this format, are assumed to have a social function and preserve order. As opposed to personal attacks, institutionalized racism "originates in the operation of established and respected forces in society."[23] Justifying decisions in education by the use of standardized achievement or placement tests, for example, is thought to be reasonable, because of the need to identify and give special attention to gifted pupils. And because these tests are standardized—unbiased in their construction, implementation, and scoring—they do not discriminate against certain persons. Any differences that are found are real and enhance the proper assignment of students and rational curriculum design.

In the recent arguments over multiculturalism, postmodernists have been especially critical of institutionalized racism. They have pursued this critique intensely because this mode of discrimination is foundational and seems rational and natural, and thus is extremely difficult to discredit and eradicate. Racism that is enacted through institutional means reflects normative expectations and, by definition, is not an aberration or unlawfully enforced. Uprooting this style of discrimination requires that its foundation be questioned, thereby revealing that the reasonableness of racism is contingent on the acceptance of a particular discursive formation. Simply put, only within a specific institutional context does racial discrimination make sense.[24] But exposing these foundational principles is usually not a tactic that has been taken by those who study race relations.

The role of what Martin Heidegger calls the "onto-theological tradition" in promoting racism has not been the focus of attention.[25] Looking for an ultimate foundation to justify worldly affairs has not been tied to discrimination. The argument in this book, particularly in Chapter 7, is that racism and other types of discrimination will not disappear until the dualism at the heart of this tradition is abandoned. The asymmetry between races presupposed by racism, in other words, has an important metaphysical element.

Postmodernists have chosen to call this exercise of power "symbolic violence." There are two sides to this activity. The first is that a particular discourse is transformed into a "dominant signification" because of a commitment to foundationalism.[26] The second is that this position of power is symbolic and not natural, and can be thwarted if the necessary critique can be summoned. Foundational symbols may be made to appear inviolable, but their source easily betrays these efforts. In short, the one act that the power of symbolism cannot halt is the proliferation of interpretation.

THE LINGUISTIC TURN

Access to a primordial foundation is precluded by postmodernism. For this reason, emphasis is placed on discourse and the symbolic texture of reality. This anti-Cartesian move should not be surprising, however, given the position on language adopted by postmodernists. Stated simply, they are known for advocating what has come to be called in epistemology the "linguistic turn." Similar to an earlier Copernican revolution spawned by Kant, this postmodern turn has altered the way in which the human presence is thought to be related to facts, truth, and other facets of reality.

While relying on the late works of Wittgenstein, particularly the *Blue and Brown Books*, Lyotard declares that all knowledge is mediated fully by "language games."[27] Consistent with this proposition is Derrida's now infamous statement that "nothing exists outside of the text."[28] Even the unconscious, declares Jacques Lacan, is organized like a language. The point these writers are making is that language is not indexical; speech does not function like a conduit. Language is much more intimately connected to whatever is known than is possible according to the theory of indexicality, argue postmodernists.

An indexical view of language is basically dualistic. Language is thought to "point to," "stand for," or "indicate" what is present in the world. Speech serves to highlight aspects of reality that may be ambiguous or partially occluded. The purpose of language is to organize empirical referents and convey these details to listeners. This portrayal is dualistic because reality is presumed to exceed the grasp of language; language, as described by Richard Rorty, represents reality.[29] If language is functioning properly, reality is recapitulated without any distortion. True to dualism, language disappears in the face of reality. What is possible, accordingly, is a literal reading of reality.

Postmodernists, on the other hand, claim that language is not diaphanous. There is, as Roland Barthes writes, no "other side" of language; there is no autonomous reality that is merely relayed by language.[30] Because of the pragmatic thrust of speech, postmodernists contend that language is dense and the effects of interpretation can never be overcome. Because "all of society is permeated by language," reality can never be directly apprehended.[31] To paraphrase Ionesco, there is nothing real about reality.

Indeed, postmodernists share Wittgenstein's distaste for metaphysics. The search for an ultimate ground is futile, they believe, because the influence of language and, thus, interpretation is not sequestered from reality. Therefore, reality is always encountered indirectly or from within the nuances of speech. Nothing is immune to interpretation. As Walter Benjamin notes, "language communicates the linguistic being of things."[32] Not even God, he proposes, is unscathed by this process.

This linguistic turn is not indicative of what Habermas calls bourgeoisie subjectivity.[33] Contrary to this theme, postmodernists are not saying that persons should withdraw from the world and turn inward. Turning toward language, instead, is a maneuver designed to engage reality in a radical way. Reality and speech acts are intertwined to such an extent that the term "real" must be rethought. Reality is simply no longer something to be verified.

Scientific and other versions of reality are the product of language games. These discursive formations do more than simply draw attention to objects, for, similar to Kuhn's paradigms, these constructs supply the boundaries of reality. Interpretation, accordingly, cannot be severed from whatever is known, even scientifically generated facts. Barthes accurately describes this situation when he writes that "objectivity is only one image-repertoire among others."[34] Most important is that facts are not interpreted subsequent to being collected, but are given an interpretive identity prior to the onset of research. Reality, in other words, is an interpretation that can demand recognition, but only by piling interpretation upon interpretation is reality stabilized and preserved.

The general upshot of this argument is that reality is not objective, a *res extensa*, but a text that is linguistically constituted. Grasping the authorial intent of this text, accordingly, is crucial for understanding reality.[35] Accurate comprehension, moreover, requires that the ways in which an author's story is contested be recognized. A text may be distorted by extraneous factors. Nonetheless, the meaning of text is never captured but read, and reading is never simply perceptual but inventive. One cannot read or reread, remarks Fish, "independently of intention."[36] Correct reading is a matter of reinventing or reenacting an author's original interpretation.

A QUANTUM WORLD

Metanarratives do not exist in the postmodern era because no language game is infinite. Implied is that the world consists of a myriad of games. "Petite narrative" is the phrase used by Deleuze and Guattari to describe these finite linguistic formations.[37] As a result, reality is crisscrossed by codes and resembles a patchwork. Each patch or region consists of a different and unique picture of reality. Moreover, each linguistic game is local because it is "agreed on by its present players and subject to eventual cancellation."[38] Regions are not simply environments that are encountered, but domains that erupt on the scene through human action.

Postmodernists cite recent developments in catastrophe theory to illustrate their conception of the world.[39] René Thom, the chief architect of this viewpoint, has argued that the Newtonian description of the universe is inadequate. Newton relies on a foundationalist principle—absolute space—to unite reality. Subsequent to the work of Heisenberg, Planck, and others, this kind of infinite domain is treated as dubious. Nothing that has a location, and thus an identity, can be boundless. As quantum theorists note, therefore, space arrives in "packets" or discrete spacial impulses.

What this quantum perspective means for Thom is that reality is discontinuous. Reality consists of a plethora of spatial domains that are sutured together at their edges. Moving from one region to another may result in a complete shift in orientation, thereby precipitating a possible catastrophic change due to the acceptance of completely different assumptions about nature or social existence. Postmodernists such as Lyotard, therefore, are proponents of "local determinism."[40]

What this new direction means is that the Newtonian universe is unravelling. The culmination of this activity, however, is not chaos, as foundationalists charge. Within each sphere rules are operative, and new norms become relevant when a move is made from one domain to another. Even the Newtonian world does not disappear, but merely represents one unique spatial domain. According to Lyotard, the universe consists of a "multiplicity of finite meta-arguments," with each one's validity restricted to a specific locale.

Given this image of reality, postmodernists write that knowledge is indeterminate. The use of this term does not mean knowledge is ambiguous or uncertain, thus signaling the onset of destructive relativism. Instead, facts depend on the action sphere within which they reside; a fact has no meaning divorced from theories, axioms, logical protocol, and other background assumptions. Facts are thus contingent, a "product of perspective," but readily knowable.[41]

Accordingly, the discovery of facts depends on phenomena that are not factual. Typically, facts are envisioned to be material objects that have empirical properties. Yet Deleuze announced that facts do not exist, only signs.[42] Facts, in other words, are sustained by interpretive components that are regularly overlooked by positive scientists. Like signs, therefore, facts must be read against the background that gives them their meaning.

There is no "zero point" that can be invoked to measure facts.[43] Accordingly, truth is more difficult to assess than in the past. The traditional correspondence theory of truth, claim postmodernists, is impossible to retain without this untarnished measure. A statement is true, according to this thesis, when it corresponds exactly to the appropriate empirical referent. But reality is no longer real enough to justify this kind of comparison. Rather than neutral, reality is regionalized and scarred by acts of interpretation.[44] Any attempt to resurrect an ultimate reality has been compromised.

Yet truth is not impossible to discern. In a manner similar to Heidegger's use of *aletheia*, postmodernists describe truth as emerging from a process of intensification.[45] The term *aletheia* refers to the idea that competing interpretations must be calmed before truth can be known. A place must be cleared in the midst of interpretation for truth to reside. There is no standard available against which truth is measured, but a perspective that delimits the criteria for determining the truthfulness of any statement. For this reason, Heidegger associates truth with unconcealedness and Fish with emergence.

Tying truth to particular conditions is what postmodernists mean by intensification. Within a particular region, for example, certain assumptions are given primacy over others. As a result, one reality becomes thematic while others momentarily fade away. Similar to *aletheia*, this process of emergence and retreat establishes the context of truth. Truth and error are thus united in the same process; a truth can always be reinterpreted. For this reason, Lyotard writes that "truth doesn't speak, *stricto sensu*; it works."[46] Similar to the turn of a kaleidoscope, different themes become prominent and provide the criteria for truth.

What postmodernism does, claims Lyotard, is to "refine our sensitivity to differences and reinforce our ability to tolerate the incommensurable."[47] Reminiscent of Planck's principle of complementarity, postmodernists maintain that different versions of truth can exist simultaneously. Depending on shifts in discourse, primacy is given to one framework or another for deciding whether a claim is true. A fact or truth is thus probabalistic, but not in the strict statistical sense. Normative statistics is a closed system that establishes a priori the criteria for specifying the likelihood of an event occurring. In a postmodern world, stating that an event is probable means its emergence is conditioned by the discourse found in a particular region and thus is not absolute.

ISLANDS OF CULTURE

Subsequent to the onset of postmodernism, cultures should no longer be hierarchically arranged. Both assimilation and marginalization, however, require this kind of regulation. Yet postmodernism denies the foundation that specifies the details of the hierarchy—who is at the top and bottom. In the absence of this uncontested starting point, cultures spread out laterally. This mode of dispersal is what postmodernists have in mind by their attempt to "decenter culture."

Consistent with catastrophe theory, postmodernists favor a "flat" organization of cultures.[48] Each culture constitutes an island with its own integrity. Gone are the ahistorical mandates that support different levels of civilization, and thus the inevitable inferiorization of specific persons. Cultures exist side by side and are free to intermingle. Clearly, elevating one over the other is not justified in a primordial way.

As described by Stanley Fish, these cultures are "interpretive communities." These associations "share interpretive strategies," and thus are predisposed to judge standards in one way or another.[49] This scenario is not necessarily solipsistic, but merely acknowledges the embeddedness of norms.

The world, therefore, is comprised of nothing but differences. Even a so-called supreme culture is one difference among many. In view of this melange of differences, postmodernists are understood to be advocates of true multiculturalism. This idea is not a contrivance that suggests all persons are the same, for a subtle form of conformism is still at work in this proposal. All postmodernists are claiming is that differences exist and none should be reduced to the other.

Afrocentrism is a prime example of this postmodern multiculturalism. The Afrocentric perspective, argues Asante, requires that Africa be viewed in its own terms, rather than as an appendage of Europe.[50] Africa and Europe represent legitimate differences, in other words, and one should not be allowed to obscure the other. But traditionally, and this is Asante's other point, Europe has been the standard against which all other cultures have been judged: The more closely non-European cultures are linked to Europe, the higher the value that is attached to these other societies. This process of Eurocentrism, as it is sometimes called, rests clearly on the metaphysics of domination that postmodernists subvert.

This notion of difference is based on the premise that cultural ideals are discursive formations. These traits may be tied to evolution, history, or some other creator of destiny, but their status as a universal is not guaranteed by such a gambit, because one mode of discourse cannot provide another with absolute legitimacy. The discourse on evolution, for example, does not have the universality required to dictate the terms of racial inferiority. Again, because traits are regionalized, their idealization is limited.

Postmodernists contend that civilization is not moving along a single path which culminates in an order where all differences are reconciled. Such homogeneity is not necessarily the motivating force of history. Instead, assimilation is the product of a desire for domination and nothing more. One discursive formation is made to appear ideal and worthy of universal emulation, and therefore is imposed on others. Various forms of force may even be employed to instill this outlook, but, in the end, cultural ideals are social inventions and difficult to universalize without extreme and contradictory methods.

As Foucault describes, cultures "irrupt."[51] No culture, in other words, has an ultimate cause or destiny. There is no *raison d'être* that orders cultures along the path of civilization. Instead, world cultures comprise a montage, with each one adding something unique to the final composite, and if a montage is going to be successful, each part must be autonomous. Clearly this is a lesson that should be applied to the development of pluralism.

NOTES

1. Jean-François Lyotard, *The Postmodern Condition* (Minneapolis: University of Minnesota Press, 1984), xxiv.

2. Ibid., 37.

3. Ibid., xxiv.

4. Jacques Derrida, *Writing and Difference* (Chicago: University of Chicago Press, 1978), 278–280.

5. Ibid., 282.

6. Michel Foucault, *The Archaeology of Knowledge* (London: Routledge, 1989), 42.

7. Ibid., 38.

8. Georges Bataille, *Visions of Excess* (Minneapolis: University of Minnesota Press, 1985), 5–9.

9. Michel Foucault, *The Birth of the Clinic* (New York: Vintage Books, 1975), 8.

10. Lyotard, *The Postmodern Condition*, 12.

11. Karl Marx and Frederick Engels, *The German Ideology* (Moscow: Progress Publishers, 1976), 42.

12. Thomas S. Kuhn, *The Structure of Scientific Revolutions* (Chicago: University of Chicago Press, 1975), 10, 109.

13. Derrida, *Writing and Difference*, 293.

14. Ibid., 289.

15. Lyotard, *The Postmodern Condition*, 3.

16. Foucault, *The Archaeology of Knowledge*, 33.

17. Ibid., 4.

18. Lyotard, *The Postmodern Condition*, 64.

19. Michel Foucault, *Power/Knowledge* (New York: Pantheon, 1980).

20. Derrida, *Writing and Difference*, 61.

21. Michel Foucault, *Madness and Civilization* (New York: Vintage Books, 1973), 107–120.

22. Michel Foucault, *The History of Sexuality*, vol. 1 (New York: Pantheon Books, 1978), 140–145.

23. Stokely Carmichael and Charles Hamilton, *Black Power: The Politics of Liberation in America* (New York: Vintage Books, 1967), 4.

24. Colette Guillaumin, *Racism, Sexism, Power, and Ideology* (London: Routledge, 1995), 102.

25. Martin Heidegger, *Identity and Difference* (New York: Harper and Row, 1969), 56–58.

26. Felix Guattari, *Molecular Revolution* (Middlesex, England: Penguin Books, 1984), 168.

27. Lyotard, *The Postmodern Condition*, 9–11.

28. Jacques Derrida, *Of Grammatology* (Baltimore: Johns Hopkins University Press, 1976), 156.

29. Richard Rorty, *Objectivism, Relativism, and Truth* (Cambridge: Cambridge University Press, 1991), 4.

30. Roland Barthes, *Image, Music, Text* (New York: Hill and Wang, 1977), 30.

31. Roland Barthes, *The Grain of the Voice* (New York: Hill and Wang, 1985).

32. Walter Benjamin, *Reflections* (New York: Harcourt, Brace, Jovanovich, 1978), 316.

33. Jurgen Habermas, *The Structural Transformation of the Public Sphere* (Cambridge: MIT Press, 1993), 27.

34. Barthes, *The Grain of the Voice*, 52.

35. Roland Barthes, *The Rustle of Language* (New York: Hill and Wang, 1986), 30.

36. Stanley Fish, *Doing What Comes Naturally* (Durham, N.C.: Duke University Press, 1989), 99.

37. Gilles Deleuze and Felix Guattari, *Kafka: Toward a Minor Literature* (Minneapolis: University of Minnesota Press, 1986).

38. Lyotard, *The Postmodern Condition*, 66.

39. Ibid., 58–60.

40. Ibid., 61.

41. Fish, *Doing What Comes Naturally*, 185.

42. Gilles Deleuze, *Proust and Signs* (New York: George Braziller, 1972), 90.

43. Roland Barthes, *Writing Degree Zero* (New York: Hill and Wang, 1968).

44. Ibid., 67.

45. Gilles Deleuze and Felix Guattari, *A Thousand Plateaus* (Minneapolis: University of Minnesota Press, 1987), 328.

46. Jean-François Lyotard, *Driftworks* (New York: Semiotext(e), 1984), 35.

47. Lyotard, *The Postmodern Condition*, xxv.

48. Ibid., 39.

49. Stanley Fish, *Is There A Text In This Class?* (Cambridge, Mass.: Harvard University Press, 1980), 171, 241.

50. Molefi Kete Asante, *Kemet, Afrocentricity and Knowledge* (Trenton, N.J.: Africa World Press, 1992), 31.

51. Foucault, *The Archaeology of Knowledge*, 25.

Chapter 3

The Decentering of Identity

INTRODUCTION: DUALISM AND ESSENTIALISM

As discussed in Chapter 1, the Western intellectual tradition has been overwhelmingly dualistic. Both natural and social phenomena are thought to be governed by principles that are not subject to human control. Identity is no exception to this rule. An autonomous element, in other words, has been sought to guide personal development. Universal standards are thus available to assess the adequacy of any identity.

The idea that human beings have the ability to plan their own existence has been, until recently, considered to be absurd. Since factors such as passion, jealousy, and greed are often linked directly to the human element, individuals have not been trusted to guide society. There has been a perennial search to ground knowledge and order on a foundation that is ahistorical, objective, and eternal. Clearly, this way of understanding human existence reflects dualism where the knower and the known are undeniably bifurcated; knowledge, as Lyotard says, is externalized.[1]

As a result, writes Paul de Man, persons have been in constant search to ground their identity on "the One, the Good, and the True."[2] Establishing identity on such an absolute principle has culminated in essentialism. Essentialists believe that a person's or group's identity has an a priori core which allows this designation to be distinguished categorically from all others. Traditionally, however, this foundation has allowed the label of superior or inferior to be applied to persons with no difficulty. After all, an identity is unambiguous and reflects fundamental criteria; interpretation has nothing to do with how persons are understood.

Given the anti-dualist stance of postmodernists, they reject essentialism. In short, there is no place for the necessary absolutes to reside divorced from the uncertainty of interpretation. Postmodernists, accordingly, decenter identity. Rather than associated with a primordial core, identity is situated and linked to a host of social considerations. Identity is made, as Simone de Beauvoir states, rather than based on innate factors.[3] No race, therefore, has a biologically or culturally predisposed fate.

ESSENTIALISM AND IDENTITY

In addressing how a just society can be sustained, Plato argues that persons must be faithful to indubitable referents for truth, which he calls Forms.[4] Because they reflect pure knowledge, Forms are thought to be superior to anything associated with daily existence. Therefore, Plato assumes that Forms provide a reliable framework that "regulates interpersonal relationships, but is unaffected by human desire."[5] In order to adjust properly to this scheme, persons have to achieve insight into their essential identity. Clearly stated, in order for society to maintain a state of equilibrium, persons must not transgress the boundaries prescribed by their natural roles. Chaos, according to Plato, erupts when there is a misalignment between persons' roles and their natural abilities. In other words, when persons try to perform roles that are inconsistent with their essences, disruption results. In order to avert disorder, persons have to understand their true identity.

According to Plato, the reason why the Athenian democratic assembly did not support a just society is that the city was governed by those who were fundamentally incapable of ruling. Simply put, people other than philosophers made up the assembly, which spawned ambivalence toward the nature of justice. A city not governed by philosophers is likely to be corrupt, since those in power will be interested in pursuing their own aims rather than the common good.[6] To be sure, the assembly was an ensemble of many persons devoid of the virtues inherent to philosophers.[7]

The way to rectify this situation, Plato notes, is to identify and properly align personal identity, natural ability, and social position. Invoking Socrates' understanding of human hierarchy, Plato argues that justice "requires that unequal men receive unequal honors and unequal shares in ruling."[8] And since this type of hierarchy is designed by nature, the resulting social arrangement is both virtuous and functional. Therefore, in order to have a good life and a properly functioning society, identity must be grounded in nature, which is true and eternal.

Plato asserts that, based on natural abilities, human beings are categorized into three distinct classes. Using unique symbolism, Plato identifies the three classes as rulers, warriors, and artisans.[9] Men of gold are the rulers; men of silver are the fighters; and men of bronze and iron are the farmers. Clearly, a caste system is formed where a specific group of people is thought to be inherently superior to others. This type of hierarchy is justified by nature, thereby removing any doubts about the arbitrariness of social order. In short, since the philosophers' reign is guided by reason, one of the key virtues associated with the Forms, a just society arises automatically. In this sense, the problem of social order is solved when persons understand the immutable character of their identity and accept their proper position in life. Ultimately, when persons accept this law of nature, society becomes stable and harmonious.

While Plato justified his classification of people with reference to the Forms, others like Aristotle invoked "universal law" and the "organismic analogy" to support their claim that certain groups of people are a priori superior to others. Slaves are obviously inferior to their masters, in a manner similar to the way in which women are subordinate to men. But this bifurcation of superior and inferior between men and women and masters and slaves is believed to be a part of the design of the universe, in which each group provides a specific function in society that promotes the survival of the whole.[10] Nevertheless, similar to Plato, Aristotle views identity to be immutable.

RACE, IDENTITY, AND HIERARCHY

The type of dualistic ontology offered by early Greek thinkers continued to dominate Western philosophy. During the Medieval era, celebrities like St. Augustine, Gregory the Great, and Thomas Aquinas supported the idea that the prevailing social hierarchy is based on a "natural condition ordained by God."[11] Through "faith," humans are able to understand their respective position in life, and their social position is thought to be a direct outgrowth of their inherent nature. Those who have the attributes to understand god are given automatically a seignorial position. Thus, a hierarchical scale is formed: Those who are capable of understanding God are closest to this divinity. A just society reflects these distinctions.

Writers during the Enlightenment Period replaced religion with reason to secure human identity and the proper place of persons in society, while a Cartesian-inspired system was designed for this purpose. During this period, however, race became the focal point of identity and identification.[12] Specifically, Europeans were no longer using religious dogma to measure the degree of barbarism of non-European peoples.[13] Instead, Westerners began to view the people throughout the rest of the world through the prism of race.

Although an argument could be made, solely on economic grounds, that black slaves were dehumanized in order to be bought and sold as objects, this dehumanization was substantiated by a logic other than economics. Slaves were not considered to be only the property that accrued to the victors of the wars that justified colonial expansion; black slavery was not solely the consequence of Africans losing battles with Europeans. For if the Europeans' sole purpose in instituting slavery was to acquire surplus labor, other people could have been targeted at the same rate as Africans.[14] Obviously, this was not the case. Therefore, what logic justified the massive slavery of Africans?

While economic and political motives are generally linked with Western expansion and colonialization, the rise of racialization gave legitimacy to enslavement. By the middle of the 1600s, European philosophers were already categorizing human beings in racial terms. Closely resembling Plato's caste system, Europeans were identifying blacks and Indians as different "breeds" or "stocks" who had inferior traits, capacities, and talents. A racial hierarchy was formed based on alleged inherent characteristics of groups.

While the ownership of blacks was rationalized through "just wars," the enslavement of blacks was legitimized by invoking racial differences. Simply stated, Europeans justified black slavery as reflecting a natural order in which barbarism and brutishness had to be domesticated by those who are rational. For example, John Locke argues that whites should subjugate blacks because Africans obviously lack the rational capacity to act like human beings.[15] Because Locke identified reason with morality, he believed that blacks should be treated like animals since they are incapable of acting morally.

Locke is not alone in taking this position on racial differences and human hierarchy. Leibniz, for example, speaks about Native Americans as if they were closer to animals than human beings. In referring to their way of life, Leibniz notes that "one would have to be as brutish as the American savages to approve their customs which are more cruel than those of wild animals."[16] Leibniz, of course, suggests that this indictment is not based on speculation, but rather on scientific evidence that explains the innate distinctions and behavioral disparities among different groups.

Furthermore, philosophers during the Enlightenment were concerned with charting cultural and physical evolution from the "prehistorical savagery . . . to their present state of civilization of which they took themselves to be the highest representatives."[17] Therefore, a subspecies of Homo sapiens was organized according to race. Based on physical and biological characteristics, people were grouped into racial categories, such as Negroes and Orientals. Subsequently, race emerged as a standard for understanding human civilization. For example, Westerners recognized the East to have language, culture, and civilization, but the Orient was also a "place of violence and lascivious sensuality."[18] On the other hand, the South, or Africa, was thought to have no culture and civilization. In fact, writes Goldberg, blacks were believed to "occupy a rung apart on the ladder of being, a rung that as the eighteenth century progressed was thought to predate humankind."[19] In many ways, blacks constituted a separate species.

Interestingly, this type of categorization was not limited to Negroes and Orientals, but included whites as well. The darker-skinned Southern Europeans were presumed to be more emotional and less rational than fair-skinned Northern Europeans. Still, all Europeans were understood to be more civilized than both Negroes and Orientals. Nevertheless, physical characteristics were linked directly to race, and race was linked directly to a particular place within the human hierarchy.

Even the idea of beauty was tied to racial membership. Because whites were viewed to epitomize human culture and civilization, they also set the standard of beauty. All the attributes that were classified under "natural beauty" reflected white characteristics. Fair-colored skin, straight hair, round eyes, and so on were equated with the common ideal of beauty, and because these qualities were thought to be racial properties, other races were considered a priori to lack beauty. Since beauty was a component of racial characteristics, those who were beautiful were also touted automatically to be superior to those who did not possess these traits. Indeed, beauty, along with language, culture, and civilization, clearly marked the lines that separated the races during the Enlightenment era. And since European culture, language, civilization, and beauty were used as the standard for assessing identity, people from both the East and the South were considered to be undesirable.[20]

Notable social theorists such as David Hume and Immanuel Kant were at the center of suggesting that races were inherently different and thus should be assigned categorically separate positions in society. According to Hume, species other than whites, especially blacks, have not shown any tangible proof of progress in terms of the arts or sciences. Even those who are accomplished in these areas are thought to pale by comparison to Europeans. As Hume states, "In Jamaica they talk of one negroe as a man of parts and learning; but tis likely he is admired for very slender accomplishments, like a parrot, who speaks few words plainly."[21] Consistent with Hume's assessment of racial differences, Kant asserts that blacks are the most lacking of all savages.[22] Kant contends that fundamental differences in color are a clear indication of the difference in mental capability between blacks and whites. Furthermore, because of their mental deficiencies there is little hope that blacks will ever contribute much to civilization.

What is astonishing is not that racist ideas were prevalent at this time, but how these philosophers gave credence to racial discrimination on rational grounds. By couching human differences on racial terms, these theorists provided justification for Western imperialism. Colonial expansion was no longer associated simply with occupying a foreign territory to reap surplus labor and resources. Instead, colonialization was now linked to a moral project: to rescue barbarians from the Old World and civilize them so as to insure human progress. This moral imperative provided justification for denying people of color "the very condition of their humanity."[23] Ultimately, in the name of universal enlightenment, the racial "other" had to be subjugated.

Paul Gilroy aptly describes this situation by declaring that "European particularism [has been] dressed up as universal," thereby guaranteeing the success of a specific political and economic agenda.[24] In this regard, the racialization of people was employed to justify Western expansion and to reinforce the position of the colonialists. Once identity is recognized to embody a priori a racial disposition, groups can be placed neatly in a social hierarchy. Once this happens, the linkage between race, identity, and hierarchy is thought to represent a reality *sui generis*.

THE SCIENTIFIC GROUNDING OF IDENTITY

While logical a prioris and the Enlightenment provided much of the impetus to supporting social hierarchy, race discourse following the Enlightenment period assumed a particular shape. During the late part of the nineteenth century and the beginning of the twentieth century, social philosophers began to shy away from classical liberal thought and moved toward a more scientific view of ordering society. In the United States, most social thinkers were interested in explaining social stratification through scientific reasoning. Many of these writers were influenced by the works of Auguste Comte and Herbert Spencer. For example, as the Hinkles' report points out, the majority of American sociologists followed Comte's and Spencer's views that "sociology [is] an evolutionary science which is a part, if not the apex of, an evolutionary hierarchy of sciences."[25] The reason for the Enlightenment was later associated with the science of evolution.

Not surprisingly, the rise of this approach coincides with the widespread acceptance of Social Darwinism in American society as the key explanation of human progress. As documented by Richard Hofstadter, from approximately the mid-1860s onward, evolutionary theory was praised as a monumental accomplishment.[26] Natural selection was recognized to be driving the selection, transmission, and adaptation of persons to culture. Similar to Darwin's classification of animals, a human hierarchy is formed according to the law of the "survival of the fittest." Races are organized with respect to their innate abilities to overcome obstacles and prosper. Those who lack intelligence, motivation, or other essential qualities will gravitate eventually to the lower end of the hierarchy. Any system of stratification, where blacks or other minorities are overrepresented at the bottom of the social ladder, is apolitical. The hierarchy found in society is simply the product of evolution.

This sort of philosophy provided fertile ground for the eugenic and racist claims that were beginning to receive attention. Despite the appeal of Social Darwinism, the effects of evolution remained mostly theoretical and a matter of conjecture. Therefore, empirical proof was required to lend undeniable credibility to evolutionary theory. In this regard, scientific research was inaugurated and consulted regularly during the late nineteenth and early twentieth centuries to illustrate the natural inferiority of particular groups of people. Similar to Europeans such as Galton, Chamberlain, Lapouge, or Zollschan, various Americans were intent on demonstrating the atavistic character of some races.

Medical doctors were among those who engaged in research designed to link mental capacity and intelligence to race. Proslavery doctors such as John van Evrie and Samuel Cartwright argued that blacks lacked both the physical and mental traits to be considered fully human: Without a doubt, they were subhuman. The proof of this, van Evrie argued, is the inability of blacks to express human emotions such as embarrassment, which is recognizable through the blushing of the skin. The blush of the skin, van Evrie argues, is something that blacks are incapable of manifesting because of their inferior, dark pigmentation. Furthermore, they lack the brain to create anything as sophisticated as human emotions.[27]

Lacking any real scientific evidence, van Evrie's and Cartwright's arguments were often considered to be nothing more than proslavery propaganda. However, the works of Louis Agassiz and Samuel Morton proved much more difficult to dismiss as political ideology. Agassiz, a prominent faculty member at Harvard, declared that his understanding of the differences between the races was the result of direct observation and contact. His findings indicated that blacks are a "degraded and degenerate race . . . [and] they are not of the same blood as us."[28] Furthermore, Agassiz believed their physical makeup was indicative of a subhuman species. As a scientist, he had an obligation to provide the facts about the influence of race so that society could be ordered according to ability.[29]

Agassiz's claims were supported by Samuel Morton's research on race and cranial size. Morton's study of over 800 skulls of different races gave credence to Agassiz's views of racial inequality.[30] According to Morton, cranial size was linked directly to intelligence. His conclusion was based on the idea that a bigger skull signals the presence of a larger brain, thus leading to higher intelligence. According to his data, whites had the largest average cranial size; American Indians were second in size; and finally, blacks had the smallest skulls. He concludes that whites have the "highest intellectual endowments," whereas blacks represent "the lowest grade of humanity."[31] These arguments reached their peak when Josiah Clark Nott, an internationally recognized ethnologist, claimed that the major difference between blacks and whites is the "seventeen cubic inches of brain that separate the lowest race from the highest."[32] Because this finding is couched in the rhetoric and methodology of science, black identity is linked directly to inferiority. Simply stated, the inferiority of blacks was proven to be an objective fact.

Following closely the assumptions outlined by Nott, Clark, and Morton, a host of modern-day sociobiologists have attempted to connect identity to biology. For example, Pierre van den Berghe argues that the unequal racial formation found currently in the United States is "deeply rooted in our biology and can be expected to persist [indefinitely]."[33] Racial inequality, according to van den Berghe, is a scientific fact embedded in human nature. In order to better understand racial inequality, persons should not focus on racism, but rather they should investigate the genetic composition of races. Consistent with the I.Q. controversy at the heart of the eugenic tradition, sociobiologists such as van den Berghe and Richard Herrnstein argue that different races have a different genetic makeup. Their position is outlined clearly by Richard Lewontin:

Different races are thought to be genetically different in how aggressive or creative or musical they are. . . . [Therefore] when we know what our DNA looks like, we will know why some of us are rich and some poor, some healthy and some sick, some powerful and some weak. We will also know why some societies are powerful and rich and others are weak and poor, why one nation, one sex, one race dominates another.[34]

Indeed, sociobiologists argue that racial inequality is only a reflection of biological inequity. Thus, if the essence of a race can be located through genetic research, these persons will have an indubitable understanding of their identity and potential. Biology is the basis of personal destiny.

At this juncture, the reader should note that while writers in different eras have used various forms of reason to justify racial oppression, all of their explanations require the acceptance of dualism. From Plato to the sociobiologists, an ahistorical principle has been invoked to support the differentiations that have been made between superiority and inferiority. The belief has prevailed, in other words, that a standard severed from interpretation is available to justify this differentiation. In the case of identity, the metaphysics of domination has been operative. Identities that participate fully in these ideals are valued more highly than those that do not. As a result, traits over which persons have no control guide their social placement; a sort of mechanical causality determines the place a person or group will occupy in the social system.

RACE AND DEFICIENCY

Whites have been associated historically with the ideals of social life. The resulting interpersonal asymmetry has had profound impact in shaping racial discourse in the United States. Because personal identity is thought to be grounded in a racial essence, non-whites have had to carry the burden of proving they should be treated as equal participants in American society. And to demonstrate that they deserve recognition similar to whites, minorities have done almost everything to resemble their white counterparts. Some have changed their names; some have abandoned their cultural heritage; and some have even changed their physical appearance through surgery.

Many minorities are committed to ridding themselves of any trace of un-American traits. In order to be included as equal members of American society, minorities are urged to eradicate their own ethnicity and adopt a new identity: one that is truly American. To borrow from Milton Gordon, an Anglo identity must be accepted if minorities are to escape from their stigma. Implied is that by accepting an identity defined as Anglo, all signs of inferiority will be jettisoned. Through complete assimilation, social acceptance may thus be achieved. Similar to the way in which Plato subordinates artisans to philosopher kings, minorities are believed to be essentially inferior to whites. Nevertheless, minorities continue to strive for inclusion through assimilation.

THE QUAGMIRE OF ASSIMILATION

While many minorities believe that assimilation is the best option available to gain inclusion, there are many reasons why this strategy is not a viable solution for achieving social equality. Assimilation places most of the burden of change on the minority without any guarantee that they will be accepted by the dominant group. Furthermore, assimilation is sequential; that is, there is no call for simultaneous change in social structure. For example, assimilation does not question the inherent inequality built into the American system of capitalism. Therefore, even the obvious logic of inferiorizing minorities for the purposes of securing cheap labor is seldom questioned. Finally, the tenets of assimilation are based on a dualistic philosophy that is antagonistic to equality. Clearly stated, assimilation reflects a racist ontology where there are two separate ontological planes of existence: whites and others. Accordingly, the assimilation perspective is grounded on racist principles where one group is automatically accorded a high status.

In addition to finding economic security, minorities are pressured to assimilate to foster a common morality. As William Bennett declares, ethnic balkanization is destroying the fabric of American society. Giving equal weight to ethnic differences has culminated in the "disuniting of America."[35] Therefore, in order to maintain social stability, minorities must assimilate to the American ideal.

The problem, according to Herrnstein and Murray, is that assimilation is not for everyone. Some groups are more assimilable than others. Depending on mental and physiological makeup, assimilation rates vary. Even liberal theorists, like Robert Park, have accepted the notion that blacks are hindered by their own physical or mental constitution. For example, oftentimes "black temperament" or a "lack of intelligence" is cited to be the major factor retarding black progress. Even Asians, according to Park, cannot be expected to assimilate fully. Similar to blacks, they differ too much from Europeans to find widespread acceptance. Moral order will not remain coherent, in other words, if these undesirable elements are introduced in large numbers into American society. The maintenance of morality can tolerate only so many exceptional cases.

The social implication of these caveats is clear: People have been led to believe that racism and other forms of institutional discrimination are no longer major problems in society. Instead, the focus is on how minorities are failing to assimilate properly. Thus, in the name of universalization and homogenization, ethnicity is either ignored or transformed into a liability. With regard to the latter, anti-immigrant sentiment is sweeping the nation, along with attacks on affirmative action and multiculturalism. The message seems to be assimilate or face dire consequences.

Are minorities left without any options except assimilation? For postmodernists, the answer is no. According to postmodernists, assimilation is not the only road to equality. Instead, social existence can be redeployed, thereby undermining essentialism and any designations that may lead to inferiorization. But for this change to occur, identity must no longer be understood to be an outgrowth of ahistorical—biological or cultural—factors. Actually, the dualistic project must be rejected if persons are to form egalitarian relationships.

LINGUISTIC CONSTRUCTION OF SELF

In *The Wretched of the Earth*, Frantz Fanon shows how dualistic philosophy has been at the center of promoting the marginalization of citizens in colonial societies. Similar to Descartes's ontological separation of pure from impure knowledge, colonizers identify white skin as superior a priori to black skin, thereby providing ample justification for repression.[36] In order to combat this type of racial reasoning, suggests Fanon, identity has to be reconceptualized in an entirely different manner.

According to postmodernists, dualism must be rejected in order to rescue persons from the adverse effects of essentialism. As Wittgenstein might contend, identity is not essential or natural; instead, all forms of identity are incomplete.[37] In this regard, he argues that there is no foundation that does not dissolve eventually into a cultural practice. There is no such a thing as an exact identity that sustains a person's or group's existence. Borrowing from Wittgenstein's work on language, postmodernists stress that individual identity is a product of linguistic practice, rather than an essence. Because language is understood to underpin all forms of knowledge, there is no place for a human essence to reside.

In a language game, no knowledge is considered to be absolute. Instead, since language can extend in any direction, a priori rules are not given credence. And because language is replete with multiple signifiers, identity based on language cannot be immutable or fixed. In this sense, Wittgenstein suggests that identity is never exact; a self-image is based on "only [the] rough approximations" associated with linguistic acts.[38] An identity never escapes from the influence of interpretation due to the ubiquity of language.

The point postmodernists are trying to make is that because language mediates all knowledge, persons are involved directly in constructing every facet of reality, including their own identity. As such, the reification of identity is made difficult. Identity, in other words, is always subject to reinterpretation and revision. And because there is no single core that epitomizes identity, an asymmetrical discourse based on inherent superiority loses credibility. Superiority, in other words, is not a determination that escapes interpretation and is obvious, or an empirically justified designation.

Identity, according to postmodernists, does not exist objectively; identity, instead, is derived from discourse.[39] There is no real self, psyche, or id that sustains human identity. In this sense, reminiscent of Sartre, identity has no destiny. Linked to linguistic practice, human beings are free to construct many modalities of identity; various identities will be lost and gained throughout a person's existence. If new rules are added to a language game, previously held identities may lose their significance.

Persons make their identities, but, to paraphrase Marx, not always according to directives they would choose. Although Barthes is right, and the "'I' is nothing other than the instance of saying 'I,'" many influences may impinge on this process.[40] The presence of power or force, for example, may play an important role in how persons define themselves. Minorities may relent and accept the need to assimilate, but even in this case, argue postmodernists, nothing ultimately justifies this course of action. The reality that sustains the urgency of assimilation is not ultimately real, but is linguistically instituted.

This way of viewing knowledge and identity is central to undermining racism, for if no knowledge is immune to interpretation, social relationships based on abstract essences lose validity. As a result, there is no justification for the hierarchies proposed by Plato, Kant, or the modern advocates of eugenics. Because all identities are invented, Foucault declares at the end of *The Order of Things* that both God and man are dead.[41] Simply translated, he is not denouncing the existence of a human element, but is rejecting normative ideals that are presumed to exist *sui generis*. Norms, and thus identities, must be created and internalized before they have any legitimacy. Therefore, no norm has the stature to dictate, once and for all, the parameters or status of an identity. In sum, Stuart Hall writes that identity is a "process of identification [that] happens over time, is never absolutely stable, is subject to the play of history and the play of difference."[42] Clearly, Hall's conception of identity is consistent with postmodernism, in which identity is understood to be a social construction that is not determined by essential considerations.

POSTMODERNISM, RACE, AND IDENTITY

Subsequent to the rise of postmodernism, Western rationality is no longer automatically universal; instead, this mode of assessment merely represents another regime of truth.[43] Therefore, discussions about objectivity, value neutrality, naturality, facticity, and the resulting absolutes commonly associated with the West are now understood to be the product of a particular narrative. Accordingly, the totalization of knowledge should be viewed to be a Western project, and not a global undertaking. Consistent with this shift in thinking, ideals are restricted and have limited validity. Proclamations about inferiority, therefore, must be enforced, because theoretically they have no justification. In the absence of overt and covert repression, identities will proliferate and intermingle without any fear of cultural or moral contamination. The inferiority recognized by colonists and other racists is not natural, but a contrivance.

Following the postmodern move that places language at the heart of social reality, a host of writers have begun to reconceptualize race. Authors such as Paul Gilroy, Cornel West, bell hooks, Stuart Hall, and Henry Gates have redefined race without the aid of a prioris. Rather than focusing on racial traits, attention is directed to examining the conditions that affect the social construction of race. In this regard, the postmodern attack on absolutes renders impotent the general outlook proffered by assimilationists. As a result of recognizing that social relationships are the product of human volition, the concept of a natural hierarchy becomes dubious. Assimilationists are thus left with no other justification for repression than supremacist ideology. A particular interpretation of race, in other words, must be made to appear inferior.

But because there is no "real self" to secure a person's self-image, this does not mean that individuals are bereft of an identity or wander aimlessly from one identity to another. While postmodernists reject the idea of a natural identity, they note quite clearly that a person's identity originates from her or his social relationships. Identity based on human interaction can be real and concrete, without being absolute. For example, the inferior status associated commonly with blacks in the United States is real, but this condition has nothing to do with biology or other so-called natural causes.

According to Manning Marable, this issue becomes clear once race is understood to reflect an unequal relationship between the members of society in terms of wealth, power, knowledge, prestige, and status, rather than some unknowable essence.[44] Therefore, race becomes "real as a social force when individuals or groups behave toward each other in ways which either reflect or perpetuate the hegemonic ideology of subordination and the patterns of inequality in daily life. These are, in turn, justified and explained by assumed differences in physical and biological characteristics, or in the theories of cultural deprivation or intellectual inferiority."[45] The point is that while black identity lacks a real essence, inferiority can be imposed through a particular narrative. Race is the product of human action, but in this case the outcome is negative.

The significance of this finding is that as long as people recognize they are created through linguistic maneuvers, they can overcome subjugation. Without a doubt, overcoming natural inequality is more difficult than challenging symbolically sustained inferiority. This is why bell hooks praises the anti-essentialist move made by postmodernists. She understands that the demise of essentialism will free blacks and other minorities from the traditionally predetermined and fixed identities that limit their range of experiences and condemn them to the margins of society.

In a free and democratic society, identity is an "open signifier" capable of assuming many forms; people are allowed to be what they choose, given in terms of their racial identification.[46] In fact, identity is simply a "narrative of the self; it's the story we tell about the self in order to know who we are."[47] Yet because social evolutionism has been such a dominant mode of discourse, many minorities have been deprived of a voice to recount their story. Basing human existence on this type of grand narrative, where all narratives are dissolved into one, is what postmodernists want to avoid. In the presence of such an ominous force, many voices are lost forever. On the other hand, in a truly democratic society the expression involved in forming an identity should not be truncated in this manner. Multiple and conflicting voices are a crucial part of such a polity.

CONCLUSION: POLITICS OF IDENTITY

Understanding identity to be a "text" rather than an essence provides hope to those who are marginalized that an egalitarian society is possible. But as long as dualism is given legitimacy, the metaphysics of domination can operate. Particular groups can arrogate to themselves a special status which enables them to claim superiority over others. In the end, minorities are not in a position to question their inferiorization; because of their essential inferiority, they cannot challenge, at least rationally, the dominant group.

Clearly, this is the case in the United States, where blacks and other minorities are thought to embody degenerative traits that are responsible for their marginalization. Writers such as Herrnstein and Murray argue that a lack of intelligence is the main reason why blacks are overrepresented in the underclass. Others, like Thomas Sowell, point to black culture as the culprit that keeps blacks in poverty. As narrow and politically motivated as these arguments may seem, these and other similar views have been widely accepted because of their link to science. In this sense, perhaps eugenicists will be called on to rank and order humans. An indubitable hierarchy could thus finally be erected.

In order to combat this situation in which groups are unjustifiably oppressed based on abstractions, identities must be understood to reflect discursive formations. Once this gambit is made, the usual justification for imperialism, domination, and subjugation, under the guise of human progress, is difficult to sustain. Discourses about racial inferiority are not privileged in any way— even when they are linked to science—and can be summarily rejected. Therefore, the integrity of difference is preserved; identity is an existential question and not a biological designation. In this sense, Foucault is correct to suggest that the death of man opens the possibility of creating a society in which persons can be judged in the absence of mandates which are touted to preserve the ideals of humanity. Because no one can claim inherent superiority in a postmodern world, identities must be negotiated. Understood in this context, postmodernism undermines supremacist ideology while establishing the basis for a pluralistic society.

NOTES

1. Jean-François Lyotard, *The Postmodern Condition* (Minneapolis: University of Minnesota Press, 1984), 4.

2. Paul de Man, *Allegories of Reading* (New Haven, Conn.: Yale University Press, 1979), 119.

3. Simone de Beauvoir, *The Second Sex* (New York: Random House, 1974), 38.

4. Ludwig Landgrebe, *Major Problems in Contemporary European Philosophy* (New York: Frederick Ungar, 1966), 126–128.

5. John W. Murphy, *Postmodern Social Analysis and Criticism* (Westport, Conn.: Greenwood Press, 1989), 5.

6. Allan Bloom, *The Republic of Plato* (New York: Basic Books, 1968), 360–370.

7. Ibid.

8. Ibid., 366.

9. Ibid., 367.

10. Aristotle, *The Politics*, trans. Benjamin Jowett (New York: Willey Book Co., 1899), 5–7.

11. Murphy, *Postmodern Social Analysis and Criticism*, 7.

12. David Theo Goldberg, *Racist Culture* (Oxford: Blackwell, 1993), 26.

13. Traditionally, indigenous people of the colonized world who resisted Christianization were seen as "veritable barbarian outcasts" condemned by God. See Goldberg, *Racist Culture*, 26.

14. This is not to argue, however, that economic reasons were not a major factor.

15. Goldberg, *Racist Culture*, 28.

16. Ibid.

17. Ibid., p. 29.

18. Ibid.

19. Ibid.

20. Since European civilization was considered to reflect the highest form of progress, using the West as the standard of measurement was thought to be rational and not political.

21. Quoted in Goldberg, *Racist Culture*, 31.

22. Immanuel Kant, *Observations on the Feeling of the Beautiful and the Sublime* (Berkeley and Los Angeles: University of California Press, 1960), 111.

23. Goldberg, *Racist Culture*, 32.

24. Paul Gilroy, *The Black Atlantic* (Cambridge, Mass.: Harvard University Press, 1993), 190.

25. Roscoe C. Hinkle and Gisela J. Hinkle, *The Development of Modern Sociology* (New York: Random House, 1954), 7.

26. Richard Hofstadter, *Social Darwinism in American Thought* (New York: George Braziller, 1959), 22, 31–35.

27. William H. Tucker, *The Science and Politics of Racial Research* (Urbana: University of Illinois Press, 1994), 13.

28. Quoted in Stephen J. Gould, "Flaws in a Victorian Veil," *Natural History* 87 (June/July 1978): 24.

29. Tucker, *The Science and Politics*, 18.

30. Ibid.

31. Ibid.

32. Josiah C. Nott, "The Negro Race," *Anthropological Review* 2 (1866): 114.

33. Pierre L. van den Berghe, *The Ethnic Phenomenon* (New York: Elsevier, 1981), xi.

34. Richard C. Lewontin, *Biology as Ideology* (Concord, Ontario: Anansi, 1991), 14.

35. Arthur Schlesinger, *The Disuniting of America* (New York: W. W. Norton, 1992).

36. Frantz Fanon, *The Wretched of the Earth* (New York: Grove Press, 1963).

37. David Bloor, *Wittgenstein: A Social Theory of Knowledge* (New York: Columbia University Press, 1983), 29.

38. Ludwig Wittgenstein, *The Blue and Brown Books* (New York: Harper and Row, 1958), 81.

39. Michel Foucault, *The Archaeology of Knowledge* (London: Routledge, 1989), 31–39.

40. Roland Barthes, *Image, Music, Text* (New York: Hill and Wang, 1977), 145.

41. Michel Foucault, *The Order of Things* (New York: Vintage Books, 1973), 384–387.

42. Stuart Hall, "Ethnicity: Identity and Difference," *Radical America* 23, no. 4 (1991): 15.

43. Michel Foucault, *This Is Not a Pipe* (Berkeley and Los Angeles: University of California Press, 1982).

44. Manning Marable, "Beyond Racial Identity Politics: Towards a Liberation Theory for Multicultural Democracy," in *Race, Class, and Gender*, ed. Margaret L. Andersen and Patricia Hill Collins (Belmont, Calif.: Wadsworth, 1995), 363–365.

45. Ibid., 364.

46. Paul Gilroy, *Small Acts* (London: Serpent's Tail, 1993), 123.

47. Hall, "Ethnicity," 16.

Chapter 4

Knowledge, Intelligence, and the Life-World

RACIAL DIFFERENCES IN MODERNITY

In a recent *New York Times* article, Lester Thurow asked, "How much inequality can a democracy take?"[1] He is concerned with economic disparity, but his question is also pertinent to race relations. In a democracy, in other words, how much discrimination is tolerable? When does depriving people of equal treatment begin to violate the basic democratic credo. This issue was raised almost fifty years ago by Gunnar Myrdal and is still relevant today.

As practically everyone knows, in a democracy the people are supposed to rule. The point is that no one is supposed to receive special privileges, neither religious leaders nor particular social classes. In other words, no one is supposed to be excluded a priori from participating in government affairs and exercising power. Direction and consent, accordingly, are expected to emerge from every segment of society.

Clearly, racism is anathema to democracy. This conflict is reflected in the title of Myrdal's book, *An American Dilemma.*[2] He believed that racism in the midst of a polity claiming to be democratic poses a serious ethical quandary. It is too bad that he took an optimistic stance and assumed this disparity was simply theoretical and would be naturally resolved.[3] Nonetheless, he argued that serious cognitive dissonance would arise because of the practice of racism in America, thereby encouraging social turmoil. Extraordinary means would have to be introduced to reconcile the opposing tendencies of racism and democracy.

To reduce this psychic tension, a sound rationale had to be given for racial discrimination. As discussed toward the end of Chapter 1, excluding select persons from the political and cultural process must be based on appreciably more than a whim. Depriving individuals or groups of basic rights is serious and requires a profound justification, for not treating people equally is undemocratic and cannot be easily ignored. In a democracy no person is supposed to have the latitude to discriminate against others. No one should have this much power; the right of certain persons to participate in governance is not subject to debate.

The citizens interviewed in Myrdal's study recognized the validity of this claim. Because all persons are created equal and endowed with fundamental rights, persons are not permitted to inferiorize others. The right to discriminate is not protected in a democracy. Such a right, to be sure, would threaten the basic fabric of a democratic society. Disagreements would simply result in exclusion.

But what if persons are not created equal? If this were the case, unequal treatment could be justified. Moreover, any discrimination would not pose legal or moral difficulties for a democracy. If certain persons are naturally inferior, after all, what right do they have to complain about disparate treatment? In fact, inferiors should never be led to believe that they deserve to be treated in a manner similar to their superiors. Social disruption results from instilling a false sense of hope in these unfortunate souls; expectations are introduced that can never be met. Because unlimited mobility is a central theme of democracy, great optimism is often engendered in citizens that cannot be fulfilled in everyone.

In order to rationalize racism, therefore, the subjects studied in Myrdal's book employed a variety of tactics.[4] Some believed that God created an inferior race, while others presumed that blacks represented the residue of evolution. Those who practiced racism, moreover, did not feel guilty when they assumed the differential treatment of blacks was out of their control. They are not discriminating unfairly against these persons, but are merely acknowledging that natural differences exist among citizens. Simply put, inferiors cannot demand, if logic is to prevail, to be treated the same as everyone else.

The problem with looking to God or evolution to rationalize discrimination is that these methods are speculative. As Auguste Comte argued some time ago, the outcome of a theological argument is never certain. God's intentions remain unknown to mortals and thus must be based on faith. How God relates to social order is unverifiable and impossible to illustrate. And as Comte feared, the resulting order can always be viewed as suspect and challenged.

Evolution, however, does not fare much better. According to Stephen Jay Gould, locating persons on an evolutionary trajectory is a difficult, if not impossible, task.[5] For an accurate placement to be made, for example, knowledge of the origin, direction, and calibration of this path must be available. And because this information is inaccessible, debates have raged over the use of evolution to differentiate so-called backward from progressive civilizations. Indeed, as suggested by Max Weber, the so-called facts cited by evolutionists are meaningless unless these data are couched within certain value judgments.[6] But value differences are not scientific and objective, and are typically insufficient to warrant abridging democracy.

A reluctance to absolutely justify a social hierarchy, conservatives claim, has given credence to cultural relativism. In the absence of irrefutable proof, the trend has shifted in the twentieth century away from making declarations about the evolutionary status of societies. The argument is that the knowledge necessary for making such distinctions has not been discovered. Conservatives believe this claim is disastrous, because the best and worst in society cannot be clearly differentiated. As a result, social morals have been corrupted, while undeserving persons have been able to obtain jobs and other positions in society for which they are unqualified. Immorality and this kind of misplacement, according to many conservatives, can only hasten the demise of the good life.

In order to reverse this trend toward cultural relativism and social collapse, and reestablish clear social distinctions, an updated approach to an old tactic has been adopted. Although using science to justify the differential treatment of races is not novel, following the development of modern psychometrics and computerized heuristics new life has been breathed into this strategy. Because of an improved ability to handle large data sets, conservatives have become more brazen with regard to their claims about the proper social organization and treatment of the races.

Witness the recommendations made by Herrnstein and Murray in *The Bell Curve*. They exhibit the utmost confidence in claiming to have identified racial differences, particularly the core features of intelligence. Furthermore, they even seem to know with certainty who will succeed and fail in various social endeavors. Their predictions include making recommendations about various groups of persons who will not be needed in the future. On the basis of their data, entire segments of society are rendered unimportant and quickly brushed aside.

Similarly, readers are assured by Roger Pearson, for example, that eugenics will benefit society if the present hostility orchestrated by those on the Left against this vastly improved science could be overcome.[7] Innate differences between persons can be identified so that highly valued traits are perpetuated. Through a proper selective process, the gene pool that contains these enviable characteristics can be preserved or possibly enhanced. The problem is that this scenario is based on a naive view of science which ignores most of the epistemological controversies that have been a key part of the twentieth century. That is, genes are portrayed to be self-contained, autonomous factors that may be combined to cause the appearance of a particular behavioral or physical syndrome. In other words, genes act in a manner similar to the way in which atoms or other empirical points were formerly understood to behave.

Overlooked by this portrayal is that physical properties are not divorced from the conscious activities that give them meaning. Pure *Hylé*, as Husserl

describes, does not exist divorced from the mind; this material must be organized into some form by cognitive activity.[8] Genes are not linked directly to
behavior, even if physical properties are proven to be the result of specific
genetic combinations. As will be argued, human *praxis* mediates linkages such
as these and specifies the identity and value of all physical traits. Nonetheless,
the empiricism associated with eugenics and other alleged scientific attempts
to specify and regulate human features such as intelligence makes discussions
about genes and similar asocial explanations of behavior sound appealing. In
general, claims about the objectivity of science obscure the human interests
that pervade the scientific enterprise.

CLEARING THE WAY FOR CERTAINTY

As C. P. Snow recognized some time ago, a culture of science is taking
root in modern society.[9] His aim is to draw attention to a schism between the
sciences and humanities that is becoming more pronounced. Indeed, perhaps
the humanities are being eclipsed by the sciences; sciences are producing
results that cannot be imagined in the humanities. In point of fact, information tied to science is described as hard, factual, and reliable, while the humanities are assumed to produce knowledge that is soft, subject to
interpretation, and uncertain. In any confrontation with philosophy or history
most of the public is convinced that science is more reliable and deserves
more attention.

The following question has been raised by some critics: Is the fundamental
structure of scientific inquiry appreciably different from cultural studies? For
example, Stanley Fish argues they are both mediated by theory, grounded in
assumptions, have a cultural origin, and are a part of the human project. Because there is no "pure spectator," the objectivity claimed by science rests on
an uneasy consensus.[10] But what allows science, therefore, to claim a status
superior to that allotted to aesthetics, philosophy, or history? The answer to
this query is straightforward, although somewhat problematic. Simply put,
science has been portrayed in such a way that it appears to be insulated from
the contingencies that plague the humanities.

The culture of science, in other words, has been instrumental in clearing a
space for research that is thought to culminate in certainty. At the heart of this
outlook are assumptions about dualism, standardization, instrumentation, and
value-neutrality that create the illusion that the sciences and humanities occupy entirely different spheres. Within the realm of science, subjectivity is
removed from objectivity, while a variety of tactics are employed to ensure
the direct observation of events.

At this time, for example, techniques are available that appear to be immune to interpretation.[11] Instruments have been created to identify, garner,
and interpret data that are unfazed by political, moral, or ethical considerations. Ackerman contends that this instrumentation creates the stability re-

quired to assess scientific progress; human error and other social contingencies are removed from measurement and assessment. All scientists have to do is follow stepwise instructions, and by achieving a specific level of technical competence an entire methodological system is put into action. Because of the apparent absence of interpretation, this framework appears to be closed and ultimately rational. A patina of logic, continuity, and soundness is generated that seems to be inviolable.

In the so-called computer age, this facade is easier to maintain than in the past. When empiricists such as John Stuart Mill were discussing the logic of experimentation and correlation, and Auguste Comte and Durkheim argued about the properties of facts, the presence of philosophical claims was obvious. On the other hand, when data are analyzed within the space provided by a computer, the impact of philosophical assumptions is much more difficult to detect.

When most persons think about computers they are conscious of hardware and software. Seldom are they aware of the philosophy that makes computerization possible. That data must conform to a certain image—the information "bit"—is hardly noticed.[12] Contemporary critics charge this oversight is the result of a unique theoretical maneuver. Through the use of Boolean logic and the accompanying abstract symbolism, the illusion is perpetrated that data are sorted, classified, and processed by a universal process that is unbiased. As described by Michael Heim, "before Boole, logic was the study of things referred to directly and intuitively at hand. After Boole, logic became a system of pure symbols."[13] Pure logic is operating, in other words, rather than arbitrary judgments.

Computerized science is identified by some critics as generating a "virtual reality." Insight is available that is not encumbered by human inadequacies; facts can be unearthed and assessed in an environment unaffected by social pressures. In this sense, data are allowed to speak for themselves. How can strict "empirical demonstration[s]," asks Hans Eysenck, be racist?[14] Through the use of advanced psychometric techniques, data are simply made available for everyone to see. The argument is that no prejudice could possibly be operating because data are obtrusive and do not lie.

Operating within the culture of science is presumed to provide a viable shelter from unfounded criticism. Dinesh D'Souza is apparently adhering to this position in his response to recent charges that his book, *Beyond Racism*, is a racist tract. How could such a carefully and copiously documented work be racist, he wonders?[15] According to the culture of science, such a rationale is often deemed to be inscrutable. Extensive notation produces what Fish, following Dworkin, calls a "chain enterprise," which engenders a strong sense of continuity that may obscure a dubious starting point. As subsequent stages in this history become increasingly dense as they are removed further from their origin, Fish notes that discordant interpretations are discouraged.[16] In this sense, an impressive amount of notes often creates the misimpression of comprehensiveness and profundity. Because a full range of information is apparently presented, no position is being taken.

In a similar vein, Herrnstein and Murray declare that their statements about the intelligence of blacks are "inflexibly pinned to data."[17] They go on to say that even "provocative turns of phrase" had to be avoided, thereby assuring readers of their fairness and objectivity. As mentioned, statements about taking data literally are an integral part of the scientific enterprise and are supposed to demonstrate an absence of bias. Sticking to the data, simply stated, insures that any differences found between groups are real.

No one should be surprised, therefore, by the current interest in I.Q. tests, genetics, and other allegedly realistic means of identifying and arranging the races. With this so-called hard data, correct social placement can be guaranteed, in addition to having an exact explanation for any widespread differences in social status. In this way, any drift of society toward relativism can be corrected, thus reestablishing a thoroughly rational social order.

In sum, the culture of science justifies this faith. Through standardization, dualism is reinforced, thereby creating the image that science is objective. The personal outlook of a scientist or reporter is unimportant. Individual sentiments are irrelevant when data are collected and portrayed according to the culture of science. Racism may be a motive of an investigator, but in the end the objectivity of science prevails.

SCIENCE, IDEOLOGY, AND DOMINATION

Science has been referred to by a variety of current critics as the newest and perhaps the most sophisticated approach to undermining the relevance of conscious intentionality, the self, the exercise of will, or critical thought.[18] In general, the purpose of such an ideology is to reify social relationships, particularly the dominance of specific classes. Advantage is reinforced, writes Thompson, by "representing a transitory, historical state of affairs as if it were permanent, natural, outside of time."[19] The exploitation of one class or ethnic group by another is not simply the outcome of greed or envy, but is an inevitable condition, a fact of life. This social asymmetry has a nonpartisan explanation.

In a similar manner, the process of racism is streamlined through the use of science. Hostility and the usual feelings of discomfort, for example, are removed from this mode of discrimination. By relying on scientifically produced data, which by implication are divorced from politics, any differences that are found between groups are not illusory or the outgrowth of a conspiracy. Because these facts are real, any sign of inferiority is merely a reality that must be faced. In point of fact, what Herrnstein and Murray recommend is that blacks, who they document to be inferior, be cared for in a humane way. Revealed at this juncture is their version of the "white man's burden"—superiors have the obligation to conserve the rest of humanity.

Science is ideological because of the seignorial position allotted to the information it generates. This knowledge is not contrived through the influence of theories, assumptions, or any other limiting conditions. Political machinations, accordingly, are not advanced by scientific methods. Good scientists are thorough and exact, and are simply servants of the truth. But because of this disinterestedness, science can produce, without much scrutiny, the "master symbols of legitimation."[20] Dominant values can be instituted through science in an unobtrusive way that appears to be beyond reproach. As Guillaumin describes, "groups [are made] into fetishes, frozen into some intrinsic form of being and possessing qualities which, whether flattering or damaging, are in any case eternal."[21] Science has this ability because of its alleged apolitical method.

Concealed by this depiction of knowledge generation, however, is the link between science and human *praxis*. As described extensively by Foucault, the traditional viewpoint of science is naïve, but can be very repressive. He argues convincingly that, contrary to being disconnected from values, science is positional and represents a contested realm which is replete with theoretical incompatibilities and procedural inconsistencies.[22] Science, in other words, is hardly a completely formalized undertaking.

At the heart of this criticism is the recognition that particular assumptions always guide the search for facts. A conceptual process, therefore, guides the scientific discovery of knowledge. Given this realization, a key question is who chooses and shapes these concepts? Despite claims about standardization and operationalization, these concepts have parameters and are not ideal. Indeed, any attempt at conceptualization has a focus that serves to make certain themes paramount while diminishing others. Feyerabend makes this point by arguing that measurements reflect "properties of complex sections of the historical process" rather than material reality.[23] When dealing with I.Q., for example, these shifts in attention can have dramatic implications. Different conceptual acts will have an impact on how intelligence is assessed; measurement, in short, is not a neutral activity.

The work of Alfred Schutz lends insight into how concepts operate in science. Scientists implement what he calls "second degree concepts," which are deemed to be more refined than those used by regular persons to organize their everyday lives.[24] These idealized notions, moreover, are considered to have unrestricted applicability because they are so refined and precise. Nonetheless, similar to the conceptualization of mundane affairs, these secondary heuristics embody judgments, claims about validity, and beliefs about utility. To be specific, I.Q. may be defined to reflect class, occupational, or cultural themes or other social requirements. As long as concepts are operative, argues Fish, some positions are elevated in importance while others are dismissed. In this sense, conceptualization is a winnowing process.

But what about culture-free tests? At least since the 1950s, the use of these instruments has been extolled to counteract bias. Proponents of these devices have fallen into a trap identical to the supporters of formal logic. That is, they assumed that formalization—similar to that found in mathematics or symbolic logic—results in "marks [signs] so self-sufficiently perspicuous" that they do not involve conceptualization.[25] In all of these cases, pure form is believed to be operative that is devoid of content. But Maurice Merleau-Ponty asks his readers to imagine any phenomenon devoid of concepts.[26] His point is that such an act is impossible, because no fact or event can have an identity without boundaries. And these demarcations, he contends, are fundamentally conceptual. No form is completely stripped of identity. Therefore, even allegedly culture-free symbols are implicated in a definitional framework that provides them with dimensions and a sense of cogency. Cultural freedom is thus an *approach* to constructing an image of neutrality, and the heteronomy of facts is merely an example of "presumptive universality."[27]

Nonetheless, reified claims about neutrality can be a potent means of domination. Discrimination can be "screened behind unassailable shibboleths as universalism and the objectivity of scientific inquiry" without drawing much attention to this effort.[28] After all, understanding the biases built into mathematics or computerization requires a level of education that most citizens have not achieved. Who is going to argue with a professional psychologist armed with a battery of sophisticated tests? Without a doubt, the average person will be intimidated by the testing procedures and computer-generated scores. As a result, identifying the so-called potential of students will be perceived to be solely within the purview of experts who are completely professional and above the political fray. In the end, however, particular norms are enforced that may result in the inferiorization of certain individuals or groups.

THE LIMITED CRITIQUE OF IDEOLOGY

Characteristic of an ideology, science restricts the range of critique. Immediately following the publication of *The Bell Curve*, meetings were convened around the United States to discuss the significance of this text. For example, a widely publicized panel, and one that appeared on C-Span, was organized at Howard University. Most troubling about these discussions was their relatively narrow focus.

What occurred, using Feyerabend's typology, is a "guided exchange."[29] By this phrase he means that all participants must adhere to specific standards and recognize as legitimate only certain questions and issues. Because such a discussion is usually recognized to be manageable and thus reasonable, the channeling of discourse that results is not viewed to be bad. Nonetheless, manipulation is what occurs, and a rational critique is restricted to certain parameters.

For the most part, two approaches were taken to address the racist implications of *The Bell Curve*. The first consisted of a typical critique of scientific analysis. Attention was directed to assessing the statistics and analytical models employed by Herrnstein and Murray, in the hope of discovering methodological flaws in their research.[30] Perhaps inferiority has not been definitely proved because of procedural and other technical errors. Critics could almost be heard to utter *voilà* once the statistics used in *The Bell Curve* were found to be suspect. In a sense, blacks were granted a reprieve because of a question about the legitimacy of some calculations, particularly in the absence of vital background information about how certain statistics should be used.

On the other flank, omissions about environmental and cultural influences were also raised. Elements of the standard nature versus nurture debate were present in this strategy. Some critics wished better experimental controls had been instituted to assess the effects of culture. Others simply took the position that any evidence of inferiority is the result of environmental deprivation as opposed to genetics. In both cases, the point is to explain away inferiority by invoking environment factors over which most blacks and other minorities exert little control.

The problem with this entire analysis is that the debate is structured by science. Within this context, asking about proper experimental controls is entirely legitimate. Furthermore, drawing attention to the possible interaction between variables, such as genes and cultural influences, is considered to be a sound methodological practice. It is assumed that more rigorously designed studies can pinpoint the exact amount contributed to the inferiority of blacks by genes or the environment respectively. Achieving this kind of precision will enable better policies to be formulated pertaining to who can be remediated and given a place in the society of the future.

All along, however, improving science is assumed to hold the key to explaining inferiority. The issue is not broached as to why a particular mode of conceptualization should be treated as inherently indicative of intelligence. Why should a particular theory of I.Q. be viewed as factual and valuable? Readers are encouraged to accept that a "general factor of cognitive ability" exists, and that this trait is inscribed by the genetic code and possibly modified slightly by the environment.[31] Intelligence, in other words, exists *sui generis* and has no link to how persons construct their reality.

But Murray and Herrnstein admit reluctantly that I.Q. is a construct. If they are correct, and postmodern theorists believe they are, research on intelligence cannot be neatly divorced from conceptualization and all of the activities that affect this process, such as values, beliefs, and a range of commitments. And because constructs manufacture reality, persons who use scientific ones institutionalize a particular version of intelligence. Scientific rationality is merely an *approach* to inventing reason. When attached to science, this construction and institution of I.Q. is neutralized. The language game of science, particularly intelligence research, becomes a reality rather than a game. Talk about disinterestedness, empirical reality, and professionalism is adopted to deflect criticism. I.Q. thus becomes a fact rather than a social convention. By appealing to reason, something as controversial and hotly contested as indigenous I.Q. gains respectability.[32] As might be expected, Murray and Herrnstein's concern about the conceptual base of I.Q. disappears behind a barrage of methodological claims and data.

Most important is that the language of science had to somehow gain dominance. A scientific portrayal of I.Q. had to become more salient than other approaches to describing intelligence. Here is where the rhetorical power of science, not to mention social–political factors, comes into play. Through various means of persuasion, science becomes known as the indispensable link in understanding intelligence. Through various institutional means, science becomes the unquestioned purveyor of truth. How this process works is vital to revealing the machinations of social domination. Who has the power, in other words, to transform science into a tool to support racial discrimination? How has science come to be political while appearing to be divorced from politics?

THE LIFE-WORLD AND THE CULTURE OF SCIENCE

Central to the success of the ideology of science, and in fact, any ideology, is the autonomy granted to this mode of generating knowledge. Untainted by interpretation, science is able to overshadow all other forms of knowing. But, as noted, science constitutes a unique culture. Initially this claim was portrayed to be important in isolating science from worldly affairs. Lately, however, this characterization has come to be viewed as a liability. Science, in other words, represents one cultural means among many for constructing knowledge and reality.

In this sense, science is not autonomous. Of course, since the advent of postmodernism the idea of epistemological autonomy is difficult to sustain. The dualism, in short, that is essential to maintaining the stature of science is passé. With language mediating everything that is known, science constitutes an "essential theoretical" or interpretive region. In the words of Edmund Husserl, science is a "regional ontology," a particular cultural domain with unique rules and expectations.[33]

Because of this connection between language and everything that is known, reality is not simply empirical. Empirical traits are given depth by interpretation, thereby endowing events with meaning. Facts do not represent pure *hyle* (matter), but instead have a texture that is imbued with interpretation and given significance through this activity. As postmodernists charge, perception is constitutive and selective. Borrowing from Husserl, Lingis writes that conscious "intentionality makes impressions into sensations, that is, givens of sense, of meaning."[34] And nothing escapes from this process. Consistent with this tradition, "race is not a fact, but a concept."[35]

For this reason, science is understood to emerge from what phenomenologists call the *lebenswelt*, or "life-world." The life-world, writes Husserl, is the "universal, ultimately functioning subjectivity" that extends as far as the eye can see, and thus provides the context or horizon of a person's existence.

This world is referred to as living because it is not comprised of dead empirical indicators, but instead is replete with values, beliefs, and other modes of interpretation. This life-world is the existential region shaped by constitutive experience. In more social terms, the life-world consists of the cultural backdrop that represents a particular way of constructing existence.

This living domain, accordingly, consists of many "finite provinces of meaning," or various regional ontologies, one of which is science.[36] As a part of the life-world, the culture of science represents a particular "stock of knowledge" that has a pragmatic thrust and a limited range of utility. In an advanced technological society, primacy is given to this outlook while others are relegated to a secondary position. Rather than natural, this domination is engendered through shifts in the "tension of consciousness."[37] In the midst of this multitude of potential realities, the cognitive style of science is brought to prominence through a concerted effort—including education and indoctrination—to elevate this specific outlook in importance.

Similar to any culture, scientists must be socialized. They must be trained to conceptualize knowledge in a particular manner and to withhold interpretation from the collection of data. Implied by this socialization, however, is that scientists are not value-free. Again, similar to any other culture, scientists are committed to particular values, norms, and demeanor. As a result, scientists have constructed an image of reality that is consistent with their cultural framework.

The various realities of the life-world can best be viewed as laterally arranged, and the "informing spirit" of a group of actors gives science its dominant place in modern society.[38] Relying on scientific instruments to delineate intelligence is therefore a cultural imperative and nothing more. Such demands are weighty, but not all consuming. The life-world could be reconfigured in many other ways, with entirely different criteria used to specify I.Q. Within the life-world, intelligence can be reconstructed in a variety of ways that reflect very different renditions of social necessity. Schutz and Luckmann refer to this prospect as the "determinable indeterminacy" of any cultural formation.[39]

Using I.Q. to identify persons can easily devolve into a clash of cultures. A low score, for example, is not necessarily a sign of inferior intelligence, but rather may signal the use of an inappropriate method of classification. Rather than the result of experimental effects, inferiority may be the product of misclassification that cannot be corrected by further refining the research system. At this crossroad, a larger question must be raised that relates to cultural imperialism. Why should science be allowed to determine the parameters of discussions about intelligence and the relationship between I.Q. and race? But as Jacques Ellul discusses, doubts about the overall relevance of a research program are not likely to be given credence when the thrust of a critique is methodological or technological.[40] Specifically, issues related to philosophy or ethics disrupt the efficiency of *techné* and are usually eschewed. On the other hand, methodological queries presuppose the legitimacy of the system in use, and are thus only superficially critical. Revealing the biases associated with a particular approach to assessing I.Q., in sum, is far more than a scientific or methodological task; philosophical issues should be raised that are anathema to logistical concerns.

Similar to Weber's objection, science cannot sustain moral judgments, but the reason for this inability does not relate to any primordial differentiation between these two spheres. Instead, the problem is that universal claims cannot be sustained legitimately by science. The cause of this shortcoming, argues Feyerabend, is that "reason and practice are . . . two different types of practice."[41] In other words, science is merely one mode of practice that must compete with others for dominance; there is nothing special about science, therefore, that demands the widespread recognition of its findings. Moral superiority, accordingly, is not necessarily associated with scientifically backed proposals. Science cannot generate findings that automatically possess the universality required to be morally compelling.

SCIENCE AND POLITICS

Traditionally, science and politics are thought to be antithetical. Politics is turbulent and unpredictable, while science is rational and certain. In fact, subsequent to the Enlightenment, science has been touted to be the savior of modern society. Through the use of this unfettered means, a clear picture of reality can be unveiled, along with the guidelines necessary to produce a fair and rational polity.

No wonder many critics, especially conservatives, chafe at the postmodern declaration that science is political. Images of chaos cross their minds as the ability to make rational decisions is destroyed. Crackpots and scientists, they fear, will be given equal treatment. The general public, declares Feyerabend, has "learned long ago to identify relativism with cultural (social) decay."[42] Nonetheless, postmodernists maintain that everything is political, and science is no exception to this rule.

Again recognizing the pervasiveness of language, postmodernists argue that knowledge is never given *in toto*. In spite of the Western urge to totalize existence through the use of abstract systems of truth, ethics, and society, a complete picture is never achieved. Stanley Fish, for example, writes that having a point of view and perspectivity are not eliminated by simply claiming to be scientific.[43] Hence, science is political because the truth it conveys is partial due to the commitment of scientists to a specific vocabulary, image of facts, version of causality, and so forth.[44]

Science is political, in other words, because it "advance[s] or retard[s] itself on issues in relation to which sides have already been chosen."[45] What Fish is saying is that an act of will extends to the center of science. Fundamental decisions are made that give currency to certain assumptions and not others. A priori criteria for truth and facticity are adopted to guide research.

What could be more political than these decisions? A privileged epistemology is protected, along with the status of a particular group of experts. Furthermore, critique is defined as a way to improve science; philosophy is merely a handmaid to science. Surely, imposing limitations such as these is considered by most persons to be a political act.

Kuhn notes that the commitment to a particular paradigm may not be well informed or complete.[46] Unanimity is not required for science to succeed. Some critical empiricists, for example, may reject the idea that they are unaware of the effects of culture. Nonetheless, as Kuhn remarks, most scientists are subsumed by important epistemological constructs that make most of their disagreements frivolous; that is, reduce debate to a concern for technical correctives. The imposition of a particular outlook by scientists escapes critique; the politics of reinforcing a paradigm are thus not addressed. Even in the absence of an active conspiracy, scientists seem to agree on the nature of facts and the boundaries of responsible criticism.

But when science is thought to be a means for gathering objective facts, of course, politics is not involved in this enterprise. Actually, those who disturb this picture of science are called political and discredited. But according to postmodernists, revealing truth is not simply a matter of providing accurate descriptions. Because everyone works within an interpretive framework, choosing which one is preferable is vital to determining the nature of truth. Essential to *aletheia* is the process of actively providing a clearing for truth. Politics and truth, therefore, are inextricably linked.

At this juncture, the argument that race has no physiological justification is relevant.[47] Through various means, persons are differentiated from one another and attributed various characteristics. The aim of scientific racism, however, is to make this racialization appear to be natural. But race formation is arbitrary, because of the elasticity of language. Where does one race end and another begin? Accordingly, I.Q. is simply a racial signifier that may be reversed or canceled altogether, depending on how far linguistic categories are stretched.

This conclusion does not necessarily plunge society into anarchy. Once persons are committed to a specific mode of revealing truth, guidelines are available for everyone to follow. Subsequent to the inculcation of the scientific outlook, for example, a clear framework is provided for pursuing knowledge. This understanding, moreover, is usually recognized to be indicative of a noncontingent reality. In modern society the consensus reached by scientists has come to be viewed almost as a universal imperative. In this sense, the rhetoric of science is extremely effective in creating a stable research format, including variables such as race and intelligence.

For those who are interested in race relations, what message should be gleaned from the foregoing discussion? Most important, science is grounded in a style of rhetoric that is designed to persuade persons to accept a particular rendition of reality. When dealing with I.Q. and other ways of identifying persons, the rhetorical base of these strategies should be recognized.[48] As a result of this insight, persons will not likely become automatically enamored of certain findings just because these data have been scientifically gathered. Questions of relevance will become as prominent as ones related to rigor, and, in terms of postmodernism, relevance is linked directly to fairness and accurate understanding. Competent researchers, claim postmodernists, do not overlook this association.

Furthermore, the awareness should be promoted that science is not inherently important. Why is scientific discourse viewed to be more significant than other modes of explanation? How has this shift in orientation been orchestrated? In other words, the current fate of scientific inquiry was not guaranteed in advance. Consequently, certain forces had to be involved in the promotion of science. Hiding behind the facade of neutrality, moreover, may be persons who benefit from the scientific inferiorization of minorities. These types of questions are encouraged by postmodernists because of the political nature of science. The critique of scientific racism, accordingly, should extend far beyond issues related to methodology and technique. In other words, the social and political side of science should no longer remain obscured.

NOTES

1. Lester Thurow, "Their World Might Crumble," *New York Times Magazine*, 19 November 1995, 78–79.

2. Gunnar Myrdal, *An American Dilemma* (New York: Harper and Brothers, 1944).

3. Stephen Steinberg, *Turning Back* (Boston: Beacon Press, 1995), 41–49.

4. Myrdal, *An American Dilemma*, 85, 88, 103.

5. Stephen Jay Gould, *The Mismeasure of Man* (New York: W.W. Norton, 1981).

6. Max Weber, *Economy and Society*, vol. 1 (Berkeley and Los Angeles: University of California Press, 1978), 12–13.

7. Roger Pearson, *Race, Intelligence, and Bias in Academe* (Washington, D.C.: Scott-Townsend, 1991).

8. Edmund Husserl, *Ideas* (New York: Collier Macmillan, 1972), 227–229.

9. C. P. Snow, *The Two Cultures and the Scientific Revolution* (New York: Cambridge University Press, 1959).

10. Stanley Fish, *Doing What Comes Naturally* (Durham, N.C.: Duke University Press, 1989), 436.

11. Robert John Ackerman, *Data, Instruments, and Theory* (Princeton, N.J.: Princeton University Press, 1985), 45–51.

12. Jean-François Lyotard, *The Postmodern Condition* (Minneapolis: University of Minnesota Press, 1984), 86.

13. Michael Heim, *The Metaphysics of Virtual Reality* (New York: Oxford University Press, 1993), 16.

14. H. J. Eysenck, *Race, Intelligence, and Education* (London: Temple-Smith, 1971), 11.

15. Phil Donahue Show, 26 October 1995, show number 4368.

16. Fish, *Doing What Comes Naturally*, 89.

17. Charles Murray and Richard Herrnstein, "Race, Genes, and IQ—An Apologia," *The New Republic*, 31 October 1994, 35.

18. Max Horkheimer, "The Latest Attack on Metaphysics," in *Critical Theory* (New York: Continuum, 1972), 132–187.

19. John B. Thompson, *Studies in the Theory of Ideology* (Berkeley and Los Angeles: University of California Press, 1984), 131.

20. C. Wright Mills, *The Sociological Imagination* (London: Oxford University Press, 1976), 37.

21. Colette Guillaumin, *Racism, Sexism, Power, and Ideology* (London: Routledge, 1995), 63.

22. Michael Foucault, *The Archaeology of Knowledge* (London: Routledge, 1987), 4.

23. Paul Feyerabend, *Science in a Free Society* (London: NLB, 1978), 37.

24. Alfred Schutz, *Collected Papers*, vol. 1 (The Hague: Nijhoff, 1962), 59.

25. Fish, *There's No Such Thing as Free Speech and It's a Good Thing Too* (New York: Oxford University Press, 1994), 142.

26. Maurice Merleau-Ponty, *The Primacy of Perception* (Evanston, Ill.: Northwestern University Press, 1971), 12–13.

27. Ibid., 31.

28. Robert Blauner, *Racial Oppression in America* (New York: Harper and Row, 1972), 103.

29. Feyerabend, *Science in a Free Society*, 29.

30. Richard Nisbett, "Race, I.Q., and Scientism," in *The Bell Curve Wars*, ed. Steven Fraser (New York: Basic Books, 1995), 36–51.

31. Murray and Herrnstein, "Race, Genes, and I.Q.," 27.

32. Paul Feyerabend, *Against Method* (London: Verso, 1975), 200.

33. Husserl, *Ideas*, 57.

34. Alphonso Lingis, *Foreign Bodies* (New York: Routledge, 1994), 7.

35. Guillaumin, *Racism, Sexism, Power, and Ideology*, 100.

36. Alfred Schutz and Thomas Luckmann, *The Structures of the Life-World* (Evanston, Ill.: Northwestern University Press, 1973), 5.

37. Ibid., 25.

38. Raymond Williams, *Culture* (London: Fontana Press, 1981), 11.

39. Schutz and Luckmann, *The Structures of the Life-World*, 9, 149.

40. Jacques Ellul, *The Technological Society* (New York: Vintage Books, 1964), 83–85.

41. Feyerabend, *Science in a Free Society*, 26.

42. Ibid., 80.

43. Fish, *There's No Such Thing as Free Speech*, 38.

44. Ibid., 8.

45. Fish, *Doing What Comes Naturally*, 251.

46. Thomas Kuhn, *The Structure of Scientific Revolutions* (Chicago: University of Chicago Press, 1970), 44.

47. Paul Gilroy, *There Ain't No Black in the Union Jack* (London: Routledge, 1995), 38.

48. Fish, *There's No Such Thing as Free Speech*, 172.

Chapter 5

Radical Pluralism and Social Order

THE HOBBESIAN PROBLEM

The focus of mainstream sociology, for the most part, has been the problem of social order. Talcott Parsons characterized this issue as the "Hobbesian problem."[1] His point is that most sociologists, like Hobbes, have feared that at any moment disorder may erupt. In other words, the "war of all against all" that Hobbes anticipated may become a reality. Particularly during the transition from premodern to modern society, early sociologists feared that the firm base necessary for moral order to survive may be obscured by the new emphasis placed on personal freedom.

Also similar to Hobbes, traditional sociologists have adopted what Dennis Wrong called an "oversocialized concept of man."[2] The intent of this phrase is to suggest that a dismal view of human existence has been accepted as reasonable in the social sciences. According to this portrayal, persons are basically rapacious and unlikely to exhibit any real sense of self-control. As described by Hobbes, persons are egoistical, greedy, and self-consumed, and thus should not be expected to express any concern for the commonweal.

What is required is a reliable method for insuring civility, but the consensus that is necessary to engender social harmony can be based on various modes of interpretation. For example, through dialogical socialization persons can be integrated into a community. Social solidarity can be created, in other words, through interaction that is inclusive and nonrepressive, thereby encouraging persons to adjust to one another. Consensus is reached because this discourse is predicated on mutual respect, toleration, and a willingness of persons to act in a forthright manner. Any universals that emerge are embedded in dialogue, and are dependent on the participants for their validity.[3] The resulting order is self-imposed and reflects the general will of the public. This version of order, as Sartre might say, is mature or socially responsible.

As discussed in Chapter 1, sociologists have viewed this approach with suspicion. Persons are not envisioned to be rational enough to act this way. Because of self-interest, any public meeting is more than likely to devolve into an opportunity to manipulate others. Consequently, society will lack integrity unless order is uncontaminated by personal motives. Given this belief, monological socialization is treated as the only method that will secure a long-lasting order.

According to this model of socialization, an asymmetrical relationship exists between the socializing agent and those who are socialized. Because these agents represent the goals of society, they are given almost unlimited authority to enlist conformity from persons. Most important is that the legitimacy of these agents is not derived from citizens, but is presumed to exist *sui generis*. Reminiscent of Hobbesian theory, citizens submit to a force that is described to be more rational and powerful than them. Despite having a relatively human face, the resulting order is imposed without any opportunity for criticism and revision.

Because of the Hobbesian legacy, what other outcome could have been expected? Self-governance, in short, was out of the question. The only alternative is assumed to be regulation by an autonomous system of socialization, disconnected from human control. In this way, order can be preserved without having to rely on the good will and reasonable behavior of persons. Imperatives are thus in place that are not subject to the vagaries of cultural or political processes. Society has a purpose that is immediately recognizable and not available for constant reinterpretation.

Various modern writers, such as the members of the Frankfurt School, refer to this version of order as an administered society. The self is annihilated, as Erich Fromm describes, by an ominous system.[4] As their identity is increasingly linked to certain institutions, persons lose any sense of autonomy. Critical analysis and assertiveness, for example, become disruptive and dysfunctional, and therefore are dismissed as unimportant and discouraged. Nonetheless, as persons relinquish their autonomy they receive greater security. The rules associated with order gain a sense of clarity and finality that is reassuring.

This administered order is maintained through domination. An image of order is instilled that eliminates ambiguity by subsuming every alternative within a seamless and completely integrated normative system. Interaction is relatively uncomplicated because discourse is standardized and easily managed. Yet the resulting society is correctly described by Marcuse to be "one dimensional," because unequivocal distinctions are made between norms and factors that threaten order.[5] As might be suspected, this kind of simplicity becomes problematic for race relations. Specifically, a rendition of reductionism is encouraged that may conflict with pluralism. As described by Lyotard, normativeness is compared to a "mean, or *meson*, or *mitte*, or medium, or *minimax*, in which differences are annulled."[6] The need for norms, in other words, overrides the desire to support difference.

A SYNOPTIC VISION

Describing order in this way presupposes the ability to achieve a synoptic vision. Implied by this idea is that such a vantage point is not restricted by perspective but is all-encompassing. From this standpoint, a perspicacious understanding of the raison d'être of society can be reached, and whoever can appear to have attained this vision can claim to have the right to manage society.

As should be noted, this kind of vision is foundationalist.[7] The synoptic position is pure, and thus is untrammeled by the particularities that shape social existence. Furthermore, the contingencies of daily life are stabilized and joined together by a force that is uncompromised and thoroughly rational. Continuity is thus given to events and other factors that would otherwise lack a firm identity and direction.

Several images of society have been adopted that contain the component required to regulate society in this manner. Imagining society to be an organism represents an initial attempt to supply a coherent explanation of how society operates. In this case, an early version of functionalism is inaugurated. Each aspect of society, similar to a living organism, is assumed to contribute to the survival of the whole. If an institution continues to exist, for example, it must have a purpose. Assumed by this scenario, however, is a standard that directs the growth of society and serves to monitor and maintain its equilibrium.

As discussed by Comte and Durkheim, the organismic analogy was considered to be out of touch with the times. Modern physics was on the rise and more rigor was required of any meaningful rendition of social life. As might be suspected, describing society to be a machine became quite popular. In fact, Parsons flirted at first with this sort of analogy. Although this imagery is attuned to reflect the prominent causal renditions of nature, society has proved to be much more difficult to conceptualize in this way. The calculations required to express a simple causal relationship, not to mention the linkage between several institutions, proved to be extremely complex. Another method would have to be sought.

In 1951, Parsons published *The Social System*, which represented his attempt to find an alternative to the mechanical and organismic analogies.[8] By using the systems metaphor he was able to outline the central components of a society—statuses, functions, and the links between roles—in a concise manner. But as he revealed clearly in the late 1960s, this system is arranged in a hierarchy which has a control center that is removed categorically from the purview of human actors.[9] Specifically, the source of the information that drives the system is given primacy over the psychological or social needs of persons.

In each of these images of society, the rationale for order is dictated by organizational requirements as opposed to personal or interpersonal *praxis*. A clear message is conveyed that survival of persons or groups is predicated on successful adaptation to the social system. In other words, anyone who is not well integrated into the system will be ostracized or punished once every attempt to enlist conformity has failed. In the parlance of contemporary writers, difference is subordinated to the perpetuation of sameness. Difference represents the resistance to integration that cannot be encouraged if the social system is to flourish.

Clearly, this asymmetry between the social system and persons is antithetical to pluralism. Whereas pluralism requires a tolerance for difference, integration does not. In fact, the sacrifice of the personal or collective autonomy essential to pluralism is a requirement for successful integration. With respect to this process of integration, a person or group is never viewed as unique, but is merely another candidate for socialization. Rather than truly other, as Derrida writes, persons are either actually or potentially the same.[10] Which is the case depends on the degree to which monological socialization has been successful. In any event, an authentic other is an illusion, an "empty alterity."[11] The other is either well integrated into the social system or unacceptable.

Before pluralism will ever come to fruition, new social imagery must be invented. What must be accepted is that others do not have to be reduced to the same for order to survive. Stated another way, difference must not be viewed as a threat to order, or pluralism will be truncated. Imagery must be invented, therefore, that can include diversity without losing sight of the social whole. On the other hand, the whole cannot be assumed to be disrupted by the recognition or addition of differences.

THE LINGUISTIC BOND AND ORDER

Postmodernists reject the realism that sustains the traditional approaches to order. They reject, as Lyotard notes, the call to seize reality *in toto*.[12] With language use mediating all knowledge, the version of order recommended by realists is difficult to support. In other words, a reality *sui generis* that eludes interpretation lacks the justification required for it to be considered universal. How can interpretation be automatically thought to extend indefinitely? Contrary to realism, postmodernists argue that a "libidinal bond" be recognized to unite persons.[13] The bond, as the term suggests, is intimately connected to the human presence; order is inextricably united with human *praxis*. As postmodernists say, the resulting order is ensouled or embodied.

To be more specific, order cannot be thought to transcend interpretation and control the human creative impulse. This kind of synoptic location is no longer available. Order, therefore, must be viewed to emerge from interpretation; order must have a "libidinal skin," rather than an objective facade.[14] Clearly, mainstream social theorists have eschewed this option. Society, they believe, could never survive with order predicated on such an elusive base. Order must be built on something more autonomous and thus predictable. Allowing interpretation to commingle with order, argues Durkheim, is a recipe for disaster. Nonetheless, postmodernists fail to heed Durkheim's warning.

In point of fact, postmodernists contend that the social bond is linguistic. Lyotard writes that "language games are the minimum relation for society to exist."[15] At the nexus of language games, or key nodal points, enough information can be generated and shared to enable order to persist. In the past, such a suggestion would be deemed laughable, but for postmodernists there is no alternative modus operandi. With no escape from language possible, order must emerge from within the speech situation.

Order, therefore, must emerge through dialogue and embody what Cornel West calls "communal networks."[16] There is no autonomous collectivity, but simply a linguistic link that inaugurates and perpetuates interaction. Through intersubjectivity, the mutual corroboration of interpretations, and the gradual stabilization of symbols, persons gain the ability and the confidence necessary to regularly anticipate the behavior of others. Order is thus achieved in the absence of any fantasy about social origins and ultimate realities.[17] Further, order is engendered without transforming society into an abstract totality which may eventually require the suppression of its inhabitants. Order flows from "symbolic exchange" that is local, concrete, and can be extended only as far as the viability of an interpretation allows.[18]

In the postmodern perspective, order does not control persons, but instead represents their ability to regulate themselves. A tacit agreement is made, referred to by Schutz as a "reverse epoch," not to question a particular mutually corroborated interpretation of reality.[19] In a manner of speaking, reality is simply a linguistic habit or, as Fish says, the product of a "speech act agreement."[20] A hierarchy, for example, is such a habit that is reinforced by ideology and possibly the use of force. Rather than natural, a hierarchy is a linguistically inspired and socially perpetuated myth.

THE LINK TO THE OTHER

This image of order culminates in what Baudrillard refers to as the "end of the social." Society, in other words, is no longer a thing—an abstract system—and sociality is not something that can be ignored.[21] Because persons are not categorically removed from one another, and never have been, an external mechanism is not required to bind these atoms together. Levinas writes that through face-to-face encounters, diversity can be united on the basis of discourse.[22] Without the usual abstract intermediary, social solidarity can be promoted; self and other can be bound together through a type of intimate metaphysics.[23]

Because of the mediating effects of language, however, the other is infinite. The "relationship with the other," writes Levinas, "is a relationship with a mystery."[24] He argues this point by saying the other is multivalent and difficult, but not impossible to know. The other's identity is interpretive and can assume a variety of forms. As mentioned in Chapter 3, Gilroy declares that identity is indeterminate; specifically, "blackness is a necessarily multi-accentual sign."[25] The other, therefore, must be approached with constant vigilance so that any shifts in signification and orientation can be detected.

Recognizing the other's linguistic game requires a particular practical and theoretical maneuver, often referred to as reflexivity.[26] Because language is active, speech can interrogate itself. As a result, the assumptions of any linguistic game can be revealed, thereby illustrating the limits of these presuppositions. Once this awareness is present, the other can be treated as truly alter. That is, the other can be approached as a unique mode of interpretation that has integrity and should be protected. If required, the other can be viewed to embody a set of assumptions different from that which constitutes the "I." Agreement, in other words, is not required for interpersonal understanding.

Postmodernists do not require consensus for order to be preserved.[27] This idea is a remnant of realism, in that agreement seems to require the acceptance of universal concepts or values. The particular is considered to be in conflict with the universal and must be reconstructed. In the end, achieving a consensus requires that the self and other be reconciled through the intervention of a larger system. But, as should be noted, the resulting homogeneity is not required to create order. The uniformity necessary for this style of integration is not essential for supporting solidarity. What postmodernists are calling for, instead, is a "vibrant unity," whereby the self and other are joined in their uniqueness.[28]

All that is required for order to exist, claim postmodernists, is the *recognition of differences*. Cornel West asserts that this view of order is the product of "synecdochical thinking."[29] Stated simply, a novel relationship of the parts (persons) to the whole (society) is envisioned, so that both order and particular viewpoints coexist. Gilroy, for example, refers to this version of order as "unity within diversity."[30] Most risky about this proposal is the assumption that differences provide a sufficient foundation for order. A self and other can be linked by nothing but their mutual recognition and tolerance of their respective differences, without chaos automatically ensuing. In this "transversal" order, writes Deleuze, "unity and totality are established for themselves, without unifying or totalizing objects or subjects."[31] Without the sacrifice of identity, in other words, the self and other can be closely connected.

What is the relevance of this conception of order for race relations? In the first place, chaos is more the result of a reluctance to recognize the legitimacy of the other, instead of establishing order on the recognition of differences. Actually, basing order on an absolute, such as a reality *sui generis*, does not require that a direct link be understood to exist between the self and other. In other words, order is achieved by focusing on the absolute, and thus the other, at best, is an afterthought. Ignoring the other in this way, however, usually results in some sort of personal or cultural transgression. But it is assumed by realism that everyone has assimilated to the same normative referent and difference is an aberration that does not require any serious consideration. Those who do not conform, therefore, can only expect poor treatment.

Second, difference is not necessarily a threat to order. Differences can be merged without sacrificing their authenticity or undermining the possibility of maintaining an overall pattern of social organization. Furthermore, the self and alter are related in such a manner that one presupposes the other; their identities are complimentary. Stuart Hall makes this point when he emphasizes that the "other is not outside, but also inside the Self, the identity."[32] As a result, attacking difference creates a situation where identity is meaningless, and thus the most perverse antics are undertaken to produce a sense of genuineness. Without difference, sameness is a very hollow notion. Identity makes sense, claims Hall, only in the presence of difference.[33] Trying to eliminate difference, therefore, is counterproductive.

Hence, personal freedom and having responsibility for the other are not antagonistic ideas. This claim is false only if the self is a self-contained atom which has no essential relationship to anything. But I does not equal I; instead, I and other interpenetrate each other. Freedom, therefore, is finite and always has been. Identity does not exist when the other vanishes, but only in contrast to alter. As described by Levinas, identity is engendered through the existence of "the other in me."[34]

PLURALISM AND SOCIAL IMAGERY

Postmodernists have introduced new social imagery to replace the mechanistic, organismic, and systemic analogies because these images of society tend to reify the self, the other, and any relationship that may develop between these components of the social bond. To avoid this outcome, postmodernists attempt to "decenter" society. That is, they aim to illustrate that order can survive in the absence of the usual reality *sui generis*. This practice of decentering, writes bell hooks, can "provide the occasion for new and varied forms of bonding."[35] In other words, in the absence of this center the chances for creating a pluralistic society are improved.

Specifically important, the images chosen by postmodernists are consistent with their desire for pluralism and what Gilroy calls a "politics of transfiguration." What Gilroy has in mind is the development of a polity that encourages the "emergence of qualitatively new desires, social relations, and modes of association."[36] This style of social organization constitutes a space where identities are not fixed a priori and persons are able to freely associate because of the absence of hierarchy and the usual differentiation made between the center and periphery of society. Hence, persons are able to (re)make themselves and their associations in a variety of ways.

In an attempt to lend credibility to the idea of a decentered society, postmodernists focus on jazz. Because of the emphasis placed on antiphony in this form of music, Gilroy believes jazz "symbolizes and anticipates (but does not guarantee) new non-dominating social relationships."[37] While expected to improvise, the jazz musician plays both with and against the ensemble. There is no central musical score, but various flights of fantasy that are coordinated through juxtaposition and contrast. No solo, however, is ever considered finished, and the final arrangement is open-ended. Gilroy's point is that the self can grow in a variety of directions, and is encouraged to do so, without detracting from the group.

In the case of jazz, the addition of difference enriches the collective. Through moments of explosiveness and tension a group of musicians exhibits new dimensions. This notion of integral diversity, to borrow from Jean Gebser, is found in other examples cited by postmodernists, such as the quilt, montage, and rhizome.[38] Again, in each example order is present without a center. A rhizome grows laterally and thrives without deep roots. This imagery conflicts with the tree, which is typically used to characterize Western metaphysics. In both the montage and quilt, diverse elements are joined to form a unified pattern. In all of these images, dissonance creates harmony; coherency emerges from experimentation and contrasting differences. Any arrangement that is accepted as real is thoroughly experimental.

These images are very different from those adopted in the past. As opposed to tight integration, novel meaning, motion, and contrast are stressed. But most important, these images provide proof that difference does not necessarily pose a threat to order. On the contrary, a quilt, montage, or rhizome is enriched by a new addition. Indeed, writes Susan Sontag, the aim of collage is to create "new meanings or counter-meanings through radical juxtaposition."[39] The introduction of another element simply casts the originals in a new light, thereby creating a more exciting picture. Rather than destroyed, the original pattern is expanded.

Attention is seldom directed to these "flat" organizations, yet their presence and effectiveness cannot be denied.[40] With respect to race relations, these images challenge the beliefs held by supremacists. Specifically intriguing is that the hierarchy, often cited to be a functional prerequisite for order to be maintained, is not necessary. Order can thrive without marginalizing or repressing entire segments of society to insure integration. To borrow from Marcuse, jazz and these other images announce the arrival of a "new sensibility," whereby diversity is appreciated.[41] A new order is possible that encourages spontaneity and novelty and does not elevate the form of order above the various persons and groups that constitute society.

MULTICULTURALISM AND BALKANIZATION

In recent years, discussions about multiculturalism have taken place throughout the United States and around the world. One of the fears most often voiced about this trend is the balkanization of society. The claim is that stressing difference will result in the formation of distinct and separate ethnic enclaves. As a concern for commonality wanes, society will fragment along ethnic lines and crumble.

There is no doubt that multiculturalism represents a radical position. Because of the antifoundationalist thrust of this position, there is no justification for a reality *sui generis* to unite society. Therefore, because of their postmodern heritage, multiculturalists are suspicious of any attempt to force persons or cultures into a common mold. No cultural position has the power to enforce this measure without invoking the metaphysical props denied by both postmodernists and multiculturalists. But refusing to give legitimacy to cultural supremacy is not the same as promoting the balkanization of society.

As should be noted, multiculturalists extend beyond the viewpoint traditionally held by pluralists. Pluralists argue against ethnocentrism and contend that the integrity of each culture should be recognized. On this point multiculturalists and pluralists agree. Nonetheless, pluralists maintain that all talk about cultural differences must occur within commonly held traditions and social expectations. In this regard, pluralists adhere to an element of realism that multiculturalists reject. There is no room in multiculturalism for these universals which may eventually begin to diminish the relevance of certain cultural or ethnic differences.

But clearly multiculturalists do not promote the atomism and solipsism that are required for balkanization to occur. The fear of balkanization is real only if ethnic groups are solely inward looking and unequivocally severed from one another. In two ways, however, postmodernists demonstrate that these characterizations are wrong.

First, as argued by Stanley Fish, all positions are "public and conventional rather than individual and unique."[42] What he is saying is that persons are intersubjective rather than simply subjective. In postmodern terminology, they inhabit an intertextual world. Persons live at the boundary of their subjectivity, and thus are always present to the other. There is no *cordon sanitaire* that insulates the self from the other. Even when deciding to become a recluse, for example, the other is presupposed and rejected. In the most profound sense, Lyotard writes that "no man is an island"; even before they are born, persons are positioned with respect to the other and must lead public lives.[43]

In terms of social imagery that is adopted, intersubjectivity is also stressed. Without describing society to be an abstract totality, the integral relationship between persons and cultures is illustrated. In the examples of the rhizome and montage, the lateral organization of components is obvious. As opposed to fragmentation, complementarity is emphasized. In other words, the claim is illustrated that cultures can be joined at their boundaries into a loose association which does not automatically invite disruption.

Clearly, balkanization is an invention of those who dislike the challenge posed by multiculturalism to the dominance of European universalism. Postmodernists do not reject order, but merely question the legitimacy of societal relations predicated on cultural supremacy. Those who benefit from hierarchy will not likely make this distinction, and will conflate any challenge to their exalted status with the demise of civilization. Nonetheless, steps are taken by postmodernists to avert balkanization by revealing the public nature of human existence, particularly a life whereby the self and other are linked by interpretation.

Furthermore, expanding on Fish's infamous phrase, "all preferences are principled," postmodernists show how even the idea of balkanization presupposes order.[44] What advocates of multiculturalism are saying is that acknowledging new differences creates another version of order, rather than disorder. Indeed, disorder could not be known if it did not have a particular form. The fear of disorder, therefore, is misplaced. The new (dis)order, simply put, rearranges old social relationships into different modes of association that may temper the strength of former alliances. These new configurations may be different, but they hardly lack integrity, form, and, thus, order. Charges about disorder are perhaps a ruse to conceal anger over the loss of a privileged position, but this hostility has nothing to do with a real absence of order, which would be impossible.

A RATIONAL SOCIAL ETHIC

Postmodernists want to avoid treating order as a fetish.[45] An almost magical and deep-seated attachment to an exalted "reality figure" is not required for persons to act conjointly with the other. Clearly, there is a morality assumed by this outlook, but not one that requires subservience to an absolute. Instead, as envisioned by Adorno, a much more rational moral principle is available. This principle reflects a horizontal, rather than a vertical, relationship to authority. This approach may be new, but is not inherently amoral.

Postmodernists share Adorno's view that irrational norms are "completely disconnected from [the] individual and collective ego."[46] These normative standards are irrational because they appear without notice, require no justification, and issue demands that cannot be challenged without fear of reprisal. This is the irrationality encountered by Josef K in Kafka's stories. Norms such as these strip individuals of responsibility for themselves and order, and render them dependent on authority. Reality is accepted, therefore, mostly because it exists. Regression to a nonreflective state is treated as normal; fatalism is thus the dominant social theme. That racism exists, for example, is evidence of its historical necessity.

Along with this externalized version of normativeness, a depiction of ethical responsibility is usually provided. As might be expected, ethical imperatives are also proscribed. In early Greece, for example, *Diké* outlined a cosmological order which is normatively and hierarchically ordered. During the Medieval period, *Diké* became God while society was rigidly stratified. Subsequent to the transition to modernity, utilitarian and other scientific approaches to morality emerged which allowed the common good to be calculated. Associated with these individualistic strategies, however, are claims about the inherent traits and proper social positions of genders, races, and cultures. These scientific and rational theories may tolerate apartheid or other forms of segregation to insure the common good. The locus of morality, although the individual has been elevated in importance, is still an abstraction; similar to the Greek and Medieval periods, the collective dictates the parameters of individualism.

A different picture emerges in the postmodern world. Persons are not dominated by norms, but through human *praxis* engage the other and establish a program for further interaction. Consequently, individuals are ultimately responsible for their destiny, while reflexivity is required for the other to be understood. What is implied is that persons have integrity, which is supported through discourse between the self and other. In fact, both Foucault and Lyotard refer to those who violate the other's language game as brutal and "terroristic."[47]

Furthermore, maintaining the integrity of the other is illustrated to be a viable moral principle in the social imagery adopted by postmodernists. A montage of elements is revealed, with none more important than any other. Each part makes a contribution to the ensemble which is significant and should be sustained. As opposed to a hierarchy, morality is inscribed as a collage of forces. Through polarity and tension, rather than distance and marginalization, a basis of morality is provided. This order is rational because interpersonal freedom is affirmed, rather than denied; order is co-constituted, rather than imposed; and, as should be recognized, reason is concrete and is created through collective action.

Based on the intertwining of factors present in the rhizome, montage, and so forth, protection of the other is a reasonable mandate that does not require invoking abstract universals to justify this idea. Contrary to the usual reality *sui generis*, this imperative to protect difference is concrete and is located between the self and other. A direct link between "I" and "Thou," as Buber says, is sufficient to illustrate the wisdom and legitimacy of this command.[48] The correctness of this imperative is revealed in the eyes, touch, or, in general, the humanity of the other. Nothing else is required to demonstrate the right of the other to flourish.

In modern race relations, this ethical imperative should be welcomed. Protecting the integrity of the other is translated as a challenge to cultural or racial supremacists. Race relations might finally be possible, contrary to the current state of race domination. In this regard, postmodernists are principled without having to introduce abstract universals—the bulwark of assimilation—to achieve this aim. This nonmetaphysical ethic, writes Werner Marx, supports the "virtues of sympathy, acknowledgment, and neighborly love" as sufficient to form a stable social bond.[49]

All that is necessary to erect a society, according to Levinas, is a "metaphysics of presence." As persons face one another directly—rather than dreaming about God or some other authority—they begin to appreciate their essential connectedness. They are not simply human beings, which implies the need for universal criteria to determine who is a member of this elite group, but, more profoundly, are modes of existence that are tied together. As individuals they share a common destiny; although unique, they are never alone. Postmodernists agree with Levinas that pure spirits are a myth.[50]

Why should persons want to destroy part of their fate? Although seriously crippled, those who are discriminated against never vanish. An economic or political orientation that creates persons who are incapacitated and often randomly retaliate against others makes little sense. Equally incredulous is the promotion of persons who are allowed, and even encouraged, to create these invalids. In this regard, both racists and their victims are aberrations; they are both the product of social irresponsibility. In sum, an other who has been violated becomes angry and, in the long run, may feel justified in becoming antisocial.

Institutions need to be developed, accordingly, that recognize the fundamental inseparability of the self and other. Furthermore, in these organizations any separation that does occur is understood to be indicative of alienation and something that should be avoided at all costs, for destiny is perverse unless the self and other make their fate together. When one party is alienated, destiny will be unkind; conflict prevents the full realization of anyone. In this sense, postmodernists recognize that Hegel was right on this issue. Neither the master nor the slave has an undistorted existence, although the former appears to be much happier.

The totality of the self, therefore, is found only with the other. "Only when there is an other," writes Hall, can you know who you are.[51] What this conclusion means is that racial strife perverts everyone. The "I," for example, is constantly worried about how to control the other. Moreover, the I cannot grow into the other, and thus is restricted. The other, of course, is stifled and begins to wither. By trying to create distance between persons, both the I and other are diminished. In the end, everyone loses. Why would anyone want to bring about this kind of misery? What personal greatness could be achieved by being tethered to a maimed other?

According to postmodernists, ethics is not something imposed on persons to deprive them of the personal freedom to which they are entitled. Ethics, instead, is the fundamental condition of existence. More to the point, acting with regard to the other is not optional; responsibility for the other is likewise not optional. At the heart of this responsibility is that the other be allowed to exist as an other, an authentic or unique style of existence.

NOTES

1. Talcott Parsons, *The Social System* (Glencoe, Ill.: Free Press, 1951), 71.

2. Dennis Wrong, "The Oversocialized Concept of Man in Modern Society," *American Sociological Review* 26, no. 2 (1961): 183–193.

3. Jurgen Habermas, "Toward a Theory of Communicative Competence," in *Recent Sociology*, No. 2 (New York: Macmillan, 1970), 141.

4. Erich Fromm, *Escape from Freedom* (New York: Avon Books, 1965), 177.

5. Herbert Marcuse, *One-Dimensional Man* (Boston: Beacon Press, 1965).

6. Jean-François Lyotard, *Libidinal Economy* (Bloomington: Indiana University Press, 1993), 167.

7. Stanley Fish, *Doing What Comes Naturally* (Durham, N.C.: Duke University Press, 1989).

8. Parsons, *The Social System.*

9. Talcott Parsons, *Societies* (Englewood Cliffs, N.J.: Prentice-Hall, 1966), 9–10.

10. Jacques Derrida, *Writing and Difference* (Chicago: University of Chicago Press, 1978), 93.

11. Lyotard, *Libidinal Economy*, 3.

12. Jean-François Lyotard, *The Postmodern Condition* (Minneapolis: University of Minnesota Press, 1984), 79.

13. Lyotard, *Libidinal Economy*, 11.

14. Ibid., 17.

15. Lyotard, *The Postmodern Condition*, 15.

16. Cornel West, *Prophetic Reflections* (Monroe, Maine: Common Courage Press, 1993), 142.

17. Lyotard, *The Postmodern Condition*, 15.

18. Jean Baudrillard, *For a Critique of the Political Economy of the Sign* (St. Louis: Telos, 1981), 147.

19. Alfred Schutz, *Collected Papers*, vol. 1 (The Hague: Nijhoff, 1962), 229.

20. Stanley Fish, *Is There a Text in This Class?* (Cambridge: Harvard University Press, 1980), 215.

21. Jean Baudrillard, *In the Shadow of the Silent Majorities* (New York: Semiotext(e), 1983), 25–26.

22. Emmanuel Levinas, *Totality and Infinity* (Pittsburgh: Duquesne University Press, 1961).

23. Paul Gilroy, *Small Acts* (London: Serpent's Tail, 1993), 123.

24. Emmanuel Levinas, "Time and the Other," in *The Levinas Reader*, ed. Sean Hand (London: Basil Blackwell, 1989), 43.

25. Gilroy, *Small Acts*, 39, 112.

26. Alvin Gouldner, *The Coming Crisis in Western Sociology* (New York: Basic Books, 1970), 488–500.

27. Lyotard, *The Postmodern Condition*, 65–66.

28. West, *Prophetic Reflections*, 80.

29. West, *Prophetic Reflections*, 82; also Gilroy, *Small Acts*, 101.

30. Gilroy, *Small Acts*, 116.

31. Gilles Deleuze, *Proust and Signs* (New York: George Braziller, 1972), 150.

32. Stuart Hall, "Ethnicity: Identity and Difference," *Radical America* 23, no. 4 (1991): 9–20.

33. Ibid., 16.

34. Emmanuel Levinas, "Substitution," in *The Levinas Reader*, ed. Sean Hand (London: Basil Blackwell, 1989), 114.

35. bell hooks, *Yearning* (Boston: South End Press, 1990), 31.

36. Paul Gilroy, *The Black Atlantic* (Cambridge: Harvard University Press, 1993), 37.

37. Ibid., 79.

38. Jean Gebser, *The Ever-Present Origin* (Athens: Ohio University Press, 1985), 309–310.

39. Susan Sontag, *Against Interpretation* (New York: Farrar and Straus, 1966), 269.

40. Lyotard, *The Postmodern Condition*, 39.

41. Herbert Marcuse, *An Essay on Liberation* (Boston: Beacon Press, 1969), 36-39.

42. Fish, *Is There a Text in This Class?*, 336.

43. Lyotard, *The Postmodern Condition*, 15.

44. Fish, *Doing What Comes Naturally*, 11.

45. Fish, *There's No Such Thing as Free Speech and It's a Good Thing Too* (New York: Oxford University Press, 1994), 282.

46. Theodore W. Adorno, *The Stars Down to Earth and Other Essays on the Irrational in Culture* (London: Routledge, 1994), 34.

47. Lyotard, *The Postmodern Condition*, 63; Michel Foucault, *Madness and Civilization* (New York: Vintage, 1973), 95.

48. Martin Buber, *I and Thou* (New York: Charles Scribner's Sons, 1970).

49. Werner Marx, *Towards a Phenomenological Ethics* (Albany: State University of New York Press, 1992), 38.

50. Emmanuel Levinas, *Outside of the Subject* (Stanford, Calif.: Stanford University Press, 1993), 39.

51. Hall, "Ethnicity," 16.

Chapter 6

Institutions and Institutionalized Discrimination

MINORITY GROUP STATUS

For many traditionalists, the current controversy over minority group status is very unsettling. In the past, identifying a member of a minority group was very easy. A simple numerical count was deemed sufficient for this task.[1] But now minority group status has become more difficult to ascertain; mere numbers are not adequate to define this phenomenon.

Women, for example, who constitute over 50 percent of the U.S. population, are claiming minority status. In various countries around the world, blacks are a minority even though they constitute a numerical majority of the population. On the other hand, many traditional minorities are arguing that a key element of minority group status has been overlooked. That is, until recently the ability to avoid inferiorization has not been given serious consideration. Minority groups, in other words, are trapped within a system that supports their inferiorization. Schaefer describes this condition adequately when he writes that a minority is a "subordinate group whose members have significantly less control over their lives" than those who constitute the majority.[2] Stated another way, select persons are made into a minority group; minority status is socially enforced.

No wonder this new dimension of determining who is a minority has traditionalists upset. Although traditionally social and cultural differences have been recognized, these distinctions have been viewed as natural. These differences are simply the result of evolution, fate, luck, or some other mechanism over which persons exert little or no control. Neither women nor blacks can claim legitimately to be mistreated. Their unequal treatment, if it can be called this, is simply appropriate. A minority group is merely not the majority—nothing else is implied by this status. The harsh reality is that in every society, so goes the argument, some persons are treated better than others.

Dinesh D'Souza makes this point in his books, *Illiberal Education* and *The End of Racism*. Clearly he recognizes that class and racial differences exist, but he is loath to blame these social arrangements on anyone. In his world of conservative politics, there is no class exploitation or attempt to gain benefits through racial exclusion. Any significant social differences that may be witnessed are the result of personal faults or cultural traits. No one is really actively discriminating against anyone else.

Poor people may experience the wrath of the middle class, for example, but this hostility is to be expected. After all, through their laziness or lack of initiative, those who live in poverty are a drag on the rest of society. Being black has nothing to do with the animus directed toward poor African Americans, according to this scenario. Racial discrimination has nothing to do with poverty or any other social problems. If blacks are poor, they seal this fate through their own demeanor; their poverty is not the result of any sort of exclusionary practice.

This outlook, of course, reflects the laissez-faire philosophy adhered to by D'Souza. According to this viewpoint, people compete at the marketplace and some inevitably lose. Little mention is made in this theory of conspiracies to control the market and the discriminatory practices that are quite common. Conveniently overlooked is that some groups may not have had the opportunity to acquire the resources—personal and cultural—necessary to succeed. Even large groups, such as women, are understood to have personal traits that reduce their chances for success.

Postmodernists have been in the forefront of trying to include the element of inferiorization in any definition of minority group status. They differ from Marxists in this endeavor, however, by emphasizing the discursive nature of this process even when the economy is involved. In other words, as opposed to mainstream Marxists, even the economy is understood to be a rhetorical device designed to insure the inferiorization of the working class. Through various modes of discourse, scientific as well as economic, various segments of the population are inferiorized and consigned to a minority group status. Minorities, argues Fanon, are demonstrated to represent "not only the absence of values, but also the negation of values."[3]

The size of the minority is irrelevant. What is important is the extent to which a group of persons can avoid being inferiorized. Women, for example, have been struggling for a long time to avoid this condition. And blacks in many African countries, where they constitute a clear numerical majority, have begun to reverse the trend through various decolonization movements.[4] A minority, in short, is a victim of inferiorization that is carried out with the aid of various theories, policies, and practices.

No doubt any discussion of inferiorization is considered to be troublesome by some persons. Indeed, someone must benefit from discrimination; why else would such behavior exist? And those who reap the benefits of inferiorization would certainly not want this activity brought into the open and halted. Blaming the market or some other abstraction, accordingly, is an effective way to deflect attention away from those who support and prosper from discrimination, particularly racism. Portraying social differentiations to be natural or inevitable is an efficient method to quiet criticism and avert rebellion.

Despite the current flirtation with a market philosophy, most persons recognize that social conflict is at the core of racism. Better jobs and housing, for example, are reserved for specific persons because of this type of discrimination. Race matters, as Cornel West maintains, with respect to having success in pursuing the good life.[5] In the United States, race has been regularly related to opportunity and prosperity. Nonetheless, this awareness has not seemed to stifle racism; depriving minorities of their right to freedom does not appear to embarrass a wide range of the American population. Persons are apparently not scandalized enough to demand that this form of discrimination be stopped. Unless racists are directly confronted, business proceeds as usual; and even when these confrontations occur, social and organizational structures related to racism are treated as if they are intransigent.

RACISM AND INFERIORIZATION

Typically, racism is characterized by having or expressing negative views about a particular group. Attitudes, in other words, can be considered racist. Most important, however, is the element of exclusion. Racism is thought to be present when specific persons are segregated and prevented from fully participating in the mainstream of society. Furthermore, those who are discriminated against have some characteristic that is used to justify this mistreatment.

George M. Fredrickson's recent definition of racism seems to reflect these basic elements. Racism, he declares, provides "maintenance of a privileged and protected status," through the exercise of exclusionary practices based on "defective ancestry" and other "socially-relevant characteristics" that justify moving certain persons to the periphery of society.[6] Although sophisticated enough, definitions such as this are not sufficiently focused. What is not directly mentioned, but is crucially important, is the process of inferiorization and who is able to implement this activity. In other words, who has the latitude to enact the racially biased ideas and policies that lead to inferiorization? At the heart of racism is this endeavor.

What is at issue is how certain traits come to be viewed as inferior. How have select traits come to be considered indicative of inferiority? Simply having specific characteristics is not sufficient to rationalize exclusion. Subordination is not natural, but is linked to particular group properties. An effort must be made, through various means, to cast these traits in a negative light. Physical or intellectual differences, in short, must become known as inferior, for empirical elements do not automatically carry a cultural sign of inferiority. Furthermore, who has the ability to enact this process and enforce this new identity? Implied by this question is whether members of a minority group can ever be racists. Do they have the ability, in other words, to carry out policies that inferiorize persons?

Newer approaches to racism are more specific about issues that may have been assumed in the past. For example, racism is based on the belief that a particular group is inferior. Different ethnic traits abound, and thus difference per se does not automatically culminate in exclusion. Indeed, inferiority must be asserted and justified. As part of his discussion of bio-power, Foucault makes this point when he declares racism requires "introducing a break into the domain of life," one that is not present in nature, in order to isolate and denigrate certain persons.[7]

In addition, the assumption is made that these traits are essential and not merely accidental to a group's existence. Updating this distinction made by Aristotle, the point is that these characteristics are key to the identity of this group and are immutable. For example, the "image of black female bitchiness, evil temper, and treachery," writes bell hooks, "continues to be represented by someone with dark skin."[8] Incidental qualities that can be easily changed cannot warrant this kind of wrath. Accidents and temporary defects do not usually provide an adequate foundation for discrimination.

In this regard, a metaphysical rationale similar to that used to legitimize assimilation is provided to substantiate the inferiority of a group. Scientific, evolutionary, and divine explanations, for example, have been invoked for this purpose. Through these efforts, argues Gilroy, Europe has been placed at the center of history without causing much controversy, at least until recently.[9] Most important is that the case for inferiority is moved beyond debate; inferiority is proven by sources that no persons can manipulate to their advantage. Through factors such as divine inspiration or empirical evidence, the causes of inferiority are made evident.

Finally, these beliefs about inferiority must be put into practice. Simply having opinions about the nature of persons or groups does not necessarily cause them harm. Racism, on the other hand, is harmful. Persons are often physically attacked or not admitted to particular institutions. And sometimes they withdraw from society or engage in antisocial acts. The point is that not everyone has the ability to inferiorize persons so that they are completely stigmatized and become estranged from themselves and society. Persons who lack this power may be biased and nasty, but are not in a position to cause the damage indicative of racism.

In many respects, racism has an interpersonal dynamic which is only loosely related to minorities having unique physical, intellectual, or moral traits. Specifically, an asymmetrical relationship is established between the social mainstream and those who are discriminated against. In addition, contrary to laissez-faire dogma, this arrangement is not the result of vaguely specified forces. Real people are given the latitude to inferiorize others; a unique mode of symbolically justified power comes into play in this activity.

What is most problematic nowadays, however, is that much of the public seems to have been convinced that racism does not occur at the nexus of self and other. The appearance has been created that the direct link between the self and alter in this process has been severed. Discrimination may occur, but no one has responsibility for this failing. Social forces often related to nature or human nature, for example, are identified as the culprit; racial discrimination is thus accepted as a part of life. Average citizens believe they are involved in a society where class and other distinctions cannot be avoided.

This type of naïve realism is not an aberration, however. Lulling persons into believing that racism is a product of some natural fear or aversion to racial or ethnic differences, or some other human propensity, is the latest strategy to conceal the internecine rivalry that is at the heart of modern society. In addition, portraying any criticisms of the prevailing social reality as frivolous or irrational, as Lyotard notes, is central to the success of this recent tactic.[10] Contrasting institutions and human nature in this way encourages the privatization of racism; racism, in other words, must be a basic human tendency. In the end, institutions are insulated from any involvement in promoting racism. As was discussed in Chapter 1, persons are loath to believe racism has been a part of the very institutions that are presumed to be the cornerstones of social existence.

INSTITUTIONS AND REASON

Before this approach to discrimination can be appreciated, the traditional description of institutions must be understood. Typically, institutions are understood to supply regularity to social life. Implied is that prior to institutionalization behavior is idiosyncratic and unpredictable. Anthony Giddens writes that an institution represents "patterns of social activity reproduced across time and space."[11] Institutions, in short, provide continuity and standardization where these traits were formerly absent.

In order to explain the persistence of certain institutions, reference is often made to those organizations meeting basic human needs or providing vital social functions. At different times these justifications have been called "social forces" or "functional imperatives." In each case, the aim is to elevate institutions beyond the uncertainty that is endemic to the human condition. Some assurance is provided, therefore, that everyday existence is stable and can be trusted. The patterns of behavior that are enacted among persons are thus controlled and given a purpose.[12]

This crystallization of behavioral patterns involves formalization. Actions that were formerly undertaken on an ad hoc basis are given a structure and become routine. Through ongoing socialization and reinforcement, the "institutional world 'thickens' and 'hardens'."[13] Particular choices, expectations, and desires, in other words, are transformed into social mandates. Preferences become norms. The thrust of an institution, in sum, is to "conceal the constructed character" of order.[14] Institutions, in other words, appear to be substantial and unaffected by situational exigencies.

Max Weber supplies important insight into how this transformation occurs through formalization. His important contribution relates to illustrating how regularity is engendered through the formalization process. Specifically, as a result of formalization institutions are made to appear impersonal and objective.[15] The illusion is created that institutions are comprised of units that are functionally linked, along with streamlined communication channels and an appropriate chain of authority. Conceived in this way, institutions are stripped of contingencies and made to appear predictable and ultimately rational.

Clearly, the same dualism that allows society in general to be externalized and thus given the patina of a reality *sui generis* is operative in formalization. By giving an organization the appearance of a well-oiled machine, the image is conveyed that the human element is incidental to the operation of this institution. Like an assembly of gear wheels, an institution is autonomous and methodical. Because of the existence of dualism, the escape from mundane affairs that is necessary for formalization to be achieved is theoretically possible; the drive for unrivaled efficiency and complete control can thus be realized.

Institutions are usually assumed to have a special status. They are reliable, while humans are not. And although these organizations may periodically go awry, due to political interference, for example, most often they are unbiased and operate in a routine manner. They introduce rationality and certainty into a world plagued by chronic strife and passionate outbursts. To be specific, institutions serve to mediate relationships that would otherwise be haphazard and rife with conflict. Behavior is channeled in such a way that persons are joined in purposeful if not personally satisfying relationships.

DISCRIMINATION THROUGH INSTITUTIONS

Most sociologists recognize that interpersonal racism is passé. Very rarely nowadays are bigots found wielding an axe at the entrance to a school to deter black children from enrolling, or shouting in a statehouse that "niggers" are no better than animals. These displays are discouraged, particularly in a democracy. In fact, recent research suggests that racism should be on the decline. Specifically, white persons declare themselves to be open-minded and willing to deal fairly with all persons.[16]

Yet discrimination persists. Most blacks claim that they encounter racism on a daily basis. Because of this discrepancy between what whites say and the experiences of blacks, new approaches have been adopted for assessing racism. Institutionalized racism, in short, is understood to have replaced personalized attacks.[17] Although attention was given to this idea by Turé (Carmichael) and Hamilton in the mid-1960s, a renewed interest in institutionalized discrimination has recently been witnessed.

Institutionalized racism is usually defined as discrimination that occurs through the everyday operation of institutions.[18] Buried beneath layers of rules and regulations, and sustained by tradition, discrimination becomes very difficult to detect. No wonder most whites believe that racism is no longer a serious issue. Indeed, they are not responsible for long-standing practices which they do not even understand, or for the actions of large institutions. Their hearts are pure, although the same cannot necessarily be said about all of the institutions in society. But who feels liable for the conduct of these organizations?

There is no doubt that institutions are ominous, particularly their labyrinthine networks of authority. Finding someone who will admit responsibility for a policy is almost impossible. Furthermore, uncovering the intent of a practice is equally difficult. As a result, revealing racist motives becomes a daunting task unless some bureaucrat leaves an incriminating memo lying around. Racism is thus concealed by rules and practices that do not appear to be tied to racist motives and do not ostensibly target particular groups for discrimination.

Although this subterfuge is bad enough, much more is involved in institutionalized discrimination. Given the unique status of institutions, institutional racism is given an almost inscrutable sense of legitimacy. Because institutions are presumed to be impersonal, how can they be implicated in a process that involves hate, rage, and other human emotions? Institutional racism is difficult to attack, not simply because discrimination is diffuse, but because any questions about improprieties are treated as an assault on reason.[19] Reason and criticism can never be united in dialogue. Remember that institutions are thought to represent a key defense against irrationality and disorder commingling with reason and order.

Illustrating the bias of institutional logic is especially difficult when a myriad of scientists, public relations professionals, and other experts are introduced to justify a policy. After all, these persons are often armed with a pile of computer-generated facts and figures which may be biased or inaccurate but have an aura of objectivity. How could all of these independent professionals conspire to besmirch the character of a long-standing institution? Usually, such a scenario has little credibility.

As discussed in Chapter 1, placement testing provides a classic example of institutionalized racism, but a myriad of others exist. Take depriving poor persons and many minorities of health care by making reference to the market allocating this resource. If consumers have the money, they are able to purchase the best care in the world. Therefore, there is nothing wrong with the American medical system; the facts illustrate that this institution is the most sophisticated anywhere. Many blacks do not have adequate health care because they do not have good jobs which provide health benefits, and not because there is a conspiracy to deprive them of services. The market is simply rationing care in the most efficient way to persons who have achieved a specific employment status. What is discriminatory about the market responding to different rates of purchasing power?

Discrimination in the legal system is equally difficult to unearth. A collective guffaw can almost be heard coming from whites when they hear a minority member declaring the American judicial system unfair. Despite recent attempts to politicize the Supreme Court, law is surrounded by a shroud of neutrality and touted to be above politics. This is particularly the case in the current attempt to base legal decisions on "original intent." As opposed to laws reflecting a political agenda, the claim is that a primordial rationale is available to justify all precedents and future verdicts. The impact of a law, therefore, can never be intentionally discriminatory, but instead persons merely respond to statutes differently. Law is universal, but behavioral expectations are not.

Sometimes institutions are found to be guilty of discrimination. Convictions, however, are becoming increasingly rare because proving racist intent is near to impossible. Moreover, because of the status accorded to institutions and their defenders, acts that appear to be discriminatory are almost interminably reviewed before a judgment is made. Persons seem to be reluctant to believe that their institutions are fundamentally corrupt. Such a conclusion, they fear, may undermine the rationality of society and invite *anomie*. Without the existing system of institutions, citizens are devoid of the rationality required to preserve order. Discrediting an institution, therefore, is undertaken only as a last resort.

INSTITUTIONAL DISCOURSE

Using Foucault's terminology, although in a different way, institutions are traditionally viewed to be monuments rather than documents.[20] Again because of Cartesianism, institutions are portrayed to be entities that persons must confront and learn how to manage. Concealed by this facade of autonomy, however, is the fact that real people are pursuing discriminatory policies and reap enormous benefits from this practice. Although linked to an institution, particular discourses and acts are responsible for the inferiorization that is essential to racism. Institutions provide a neat cover story to conceal the actual intentions of racists.

But this institutional autonomy is an illusion, claim postmodernists. Similar to the prevailing literary canon, institutions have a history that is contested from a variety of angles. Currently institutionalized patterns of behavior, in other words, have gained prominence through persuasion, manipulation, and even coercion. Following a contest between language games, the victor becomes gradually sedimented and acquires a sense of urgency. Nonetheless, this hegemony is never complete, because no canon can erase the "transient,

·partial, shifting, and contingent understandings" that are a part of its development.[21] Neither a canon nor an institution ever reaches a completely transcendental or universal state. All institutions are thus positional.[22]

What postmodernists want to emphasize is not the absurdity of institutions, but instead how these institutions are erected. They reflect debate, consensus, and sometimes the outcome of wars. The point is that rather than being structural, mechanical, or organic in nature, institutions are discursive. Through actual, ongoing interaction, although the parties involved are not often viewed as equal, regular patterns of behavior are established. Institutions are thus forged out of *praxis*, as opposed to representing the idealized traits most persons can never acquire.

Rather than reflecting universal standards, institutions are a human endeavor that may reveal conflicting modes of rationality. There is nothing special or sacrosanct about institutions: They have the same properties as human action; only the gloss may seem smoother. Rather than ideal, writes Fish, institutions, like canons, are "always emerging and re-emerging in response to historical needs and contingencies."[23] Institutions are never finished or complete, but are always awaiting a new humanly inspired direction.

This sort of Copernican revolution is referred to by Foucault as the onset of "governmentality."[24] In this case, the focus of order is self-governance; self-regulation is thus the hallmark of this style of institutionalization. Because institutions are simply sedimented *praxis*, persons have nothing to rely on but themselves. Therefore, institutions do nothing more than record the human biography, but not always in all its nuances. As a *dispositif*—characterized by positive investment and involvement—an institution can only be forcibly removed from human control.[25] Even then, the resulting alienation is illusory; institutions never become completely autonomous, even during periods of repression.

To paraphrase Marx, persons make institutions, but not always in accordance with their intentions. More powerful discursive formations may inferiorize others, thereby reinforcing certain institutionalized behaviors. In other words, the presence of a particular mode of *praxis* may weigh on a particular group of persons and cause their disenfranchisement from society. But even in this situation there is no ultimate justification for marginalization.

RACISM AND ACCESS TO INSTITUTIONS

Considering the antifoundationalist stance of postmodernists, institutions and the discrimination concealed by these organizations must be rethought. Because every position is principled or structured around specific assumptions, neutrality is no longer an option. Institutions are no exception. As opposed to universal reason, institutions represent a particular position on rationality. In a society that claims to be pluralist, moreover, all institutions should have a polyvalent character.

Institutional discrimination, therefore, cannot be blamed simply on the increasing size of these organizations. Perhaps, as neoconservatives seem to believe, institutions have become so cumbersome that not everyone is treated fairly. As Robert Michels argued, maybe the nature of organizations is to become gradually narrower, thereby fostering a concentration of resources that detrimentally affects some persons more than others?[26]

These answers are simply too imbued with realism to be acceptable to postmodernists. What institutional discrimination represents, instead, is the elevation of one mode of discourse over others under the guise of neutrality. Hence, cultural hegemony is exercised without any overt display of power. Linked to reason, science, or tradition, for example, the differential treatment of persons is justified and enacted. This mistreatment is not thought to be intentional, but rather is provided with an apolitical facade. Enough distance has been inserted between those who discriminate and their victims so that those who perpetrate racists acts never appear to be harming anyone. After all, malicious intent is difficult to attribute to something inert, such as an institution.

Racism and other forms of discrimination are made to appear to be a part of the natural course of events. Changing social institutions, therefore, is argued to be unwarranted. Because these organizations are portrayed by the mainstream to be neutral, any intervention is referred to as disruptive and prejudicial. Witness the recent attacks on affirmative action.[27] The image is conveyed that functional institutions which promote the commonweal are under siege by disgruntled citizens who are solely politically motivated. As a result, these organizations are suddenly succumbing to political pressure and becoming deformed. Formerly they were neutral—surviving the test of time and representing the best of humanity—and now they are being distorted by ignoble motives. Affirmative action is simply irrational and socially demoralizing, and the continuation of race-conscious solutions will create additional problems.

Postmodernists argue that this description of affirmative action is predicated on a fantasy that shelters advantage and privilege from critique. Prior to affirmative action, institutions were not neutral or devoid of pressures exerted by specific groups. Many Europeans and others who claim racial or ethnic superiority have always believed that certain occupations should be reserved for them.[28] They perpetrated theories about human nature and myths about various cultures to insure that others would be kept out of these positions. At no time, describes Fish, has the playing field been level. Certain groups have always had advantages based on income in addition to access to high culture, important educational institutions, and social support networks.[29] Only by ignoring history does affirmative action seem unfair.

Affirmative action, therefore, does not represent an effort to undermine unbiased institutions, but rather is an attempt to confront prejudice and discrimination. A conflict of perspectives is thus underway which is threatening to those who formerly monopolized institutions. Instead of morality succumbing to politics, a challenged is posed to those who want to retain control of the key institutions in society. Grousing about reverse discrimination and how affirmative action will destroy open competition is a thinly veiled defense mechanism.[30] To be sure, those who benefited from racism in the past were never too worried about the demise of morality. White supremacy was not thought to be immoral by many segments of the American populace.

Following the onset of affirmative action, competition may be encouraged for the first time. Countervailing powers will exist, thereby giving every group some leverage. Economic redistribution might then be possible. This prospect can be considered discriminatory only if particular positions and advantages are presumed to be the sole property of particular groups. Those who were formerly excluded from important networks and thus denied information about jobs and other facets of institutional life will no longer be condemned to the margins of society.[31] They will have the advocates that other, more elite groups have always taken for granted.

What makes this assessment of affirmative action postmodern? First, institutional neutrality is illustrated to be a perspective that is deanimated through symbolism. Second, as opposed to ideology, this neutralization process is understood to be rational rather than the result of overt political maneuvering or irrational propaganda. In other words, postmodernists have shown how reason can be made to appear universal and subsequently placed in the service of particular interests without drawing attention to this contradiction. In this regard, postmodernists have broadened the class analysis of traditional Marxists.[32]

The aim of affirmative action, according to postmodernists, is not merely to correct the disequilibrium that is present in today's institutions.[33] This type of corrective does not necessarily challenge the hegemony of discourse that is central to institutionalized discrimination, but may merely reestablish a status quo *ante* that is hardly pluralistic. While discussing Du Bois's strategy to uplift blacks, Manning Marable contends that dismantling racism should not require the aesthetic and cultural assimilation of blackness to white values and social norms.[34] Making blackness disappear is not the most appropriate way, especially in a democracy, to end racism. Another strategy, and one that is consistent with a democratic polity, is to decenter order, which requires that the usual view of institutions be rethought. Only by undermining the possibility of a reality *sui generis* and the accompanying hierarchical social imagery will affirmative action and other redistributive measures bring to fruition more open and equitable institutions. Only by undercutting the possibility of institutional autonomy will the ability of any group to monopolize organizations be undercut.

Clearly, this approach to affirmative action is more encompassing than the version proposed by those who want to link class- and race-based remedies.[35] At first this strategy sounds progressive. Their aim, however, is not to dismantle the control certain classes have over opportunities. Although some poor whites may be admitted to the social system along with blacks, the opportunity structure can shrink at any time because the sources of privilege are not challenged. As an example, middle-class blacks are known to experience discrimination. Gaining a modicum of economic mobility, therefore, may have little impact on the system of advantage that dictates the "life chances" of most persons. But what else can be expected when most individuals or groups do not have the power to demand entry to the economy or other key institutions?[36]

TRANSPARENT INSTITUTIONS

Rather than make institutions disappear, postmodernists want to make them transparent. Critics are correct to some degree, however, because this maneuver will certainly subvert the monolithic organizations that support institutionalized discrimination. But the accusation that postmodernists want to dismantle all institutions, as a matter of principle, is simply inaccurate.

In this case, transparency is understood in a manner similar to Jean Gebser. This level of clarity is achieved when "everything latent behind and before the world" is exposed.[37] What he means is that human action is acknowledged to pervade everything that is known, and thus nothing is preserved from interpretation. Through human *praxis*, meaning is gathered together—or "intensified," as Gebser says—and made into facts, while behavioral options are condensed into institutions. With the world mediated fully by the human presence, there is no place left for the reason allegedly associated with institutions to exist.

The metaphysical claims that rationalize institutionalized discrimination are thus flushed into the open. They are exposed to be discursive formations that aspire to a higher status than can be justified subsequent to the demise of dualism. Once this insight is achieved, racist practices are exposed for what they really are: attempts to secure unfair advantage by appealing to institutional authority. Revealed is the scurrilous activity of trying to associate the odious act of discrimination with a primary and traditional source of moral order.

Most important at this juncture is not that institutional changes are made, or at least suggested, but a new raison d'être for institutions is offered. None of the old metaphysical options are invoked to guide this transformation; neither God, evolution, nor any other abstraction is introduced for this purpose. For when any of these theories is utilized, institutions arrive *ex post facto* and are confronted. In other words, because institutions are the product of an external force, they arrive as historical necessities. Newness, therefore, is not a guarantee against the sanctification of institutional authority; newness is not a guarantee that discrimination will not again be justified.

When institutions are reclaimed through reflexivity and the exercise of language, the rationale for an institution is completely visible. Simply put, as a result of collective deliberation one behavioral repertoire is chosen over others and instituted. In societies where power differentials exist and racism is likely, not everyone may be invited to participate in this deliberation process.

The end product of this unfair condition, nonetheless, does not have metaphysical justification. Accordingly, change agents are not confronting an inviolable reality when they argue for society to take a new direction, but are merely abandoning a formidable interpretive formation. When promoting change, however, this difference is important.

This ability of language to assault tradition is referred to by postmodernists as "transgression."[38] The radical nature of language extends to the core of speech acts; linguistic acts are unstable and continually attract further investigation. Institutions that are snared within this activity can never attain the status coveted by realists. Because language crisscrosses reality and thus infects institutional imperatives, racial discrimination loses the support of institutions.[39] Through acts of linguistic transgression, old visions can be erased and new ones created. Racism is thus a norm that can be canceled, although the memory of this discrimination remains intact.

Tradition is thus modified without destroying a sense of history. The past does not disappear, even though any former period loses its ability to dictate the future. In this regard, historical determinism is undermined, while a sense of continuity with the past is maintained. Again, contrary to what conservatives claim, the postmodern critique of an institutional presence does not necessarily culminate in a state of disorientation. Rather, as Albert Camus explains in *The Rebel*, the point is to give a new direction to history, to have persons recall the past to make a different future, and to give persons the control to remake their biographies and the corresponding institutions.[40] Institutions, and thus entire traditions, can be redirected without the threat of chaos.

NOTES

1. Richard Schaefer, *Race and Ethnicity in the United States* (New York: Harper Collins, 1995), 4.
2. Ibid., 6.
3. Frantz Fanon, *The Wretched of the Earth* (New York: Grove Press, 1963), 41.
4. Ibid., 36.
5. Cornel West, *Race Matters* (Boston: Beacon Press, 1993), 155.
6. Quoted in Vernon J. Williams, Jr., *Rethinking Race* (Lexington: University of Kentucky Press, 1996), 5.
7. Michel Foucault, "Faire vivre et laisser mourir: la maissance du racisme," *Les Temps Modernes* 535 (February 1991): 53.
8. bell hooks, *Killing Rage* (New York: Henry Holt and Company, 1995), 127.
9. Paul Gilroy, *The Black Atlantic* (Cambridge: Harvard University Press, 1993), 190.
10. Jean François Lyotard, *The Postmodern Condition* (Minneapolis: University of Minnesota Press, 1984), 75.
11. Anthony Giddens, *Sociology* (New York: Harcourt Brace Jovanovich, 1987), 11.
12. Peter Berger and Thomas Luckmann, *The Social Construction of Reality* (New York: Doubleday, 1967), 54–55.
13. Ibid., 59.

14. Peter L. Berger, *The Sacred Canopy* (Garden City, N.Y.: Doubleday, 1969), 33.

15. Berger and Luckmann, *The Social Construction of Reality*, 59.

16. Gerald David Jaynes and Robin M. Williams, Jr., *A Common Destiny: Blacks and American Society* (Washington, D.C.: National Academy Press, 1989), 115–160.

17. hooks, *Killing Rage*, 5.

18. Daniel J. Curran and Claire M. Renzetti, *Social Problems* (Boston: Allyn and Bacon, 1996), 126.

19. Michel Foucault, *Madness and Civilization* (New York: Vintage Books, 1973), 250.

20. Michel Foucault, *The Archaeology of Knowledge* (London: Routledge, 1989), 138–139.

21. Stanley Fish, "The Common Touch, or, One Size Fits All," in *The Politics of Liberal Education*, ed. Darryl J. Gless and Barbara Herrnstein Smith (Durham, N.C.: Duke University Press, 1992), 251.

22. James A. Banks, "The Canon Debate, Knowledge Construction, and Multicultural Education," in *Multicultural Education, Transformative Knowledge, and Action*, ed. James A. Banks (New York: Teachers College Press, 1996), 6–8.

23. Fish, "The Common Touch," 261.

24. Michel Foucault, "Governmentality," in *The Foucault Effect*, ed. Graham Burchell, Colin Gordon, and Peter Miller (Chicago: University of Chicago Press, 1991), 87–104.

25. Jean François Lyotard, *Libidinal Economy* (Bloomington: Indiana University Press, 1993), 5.

26. Robert Michels, *Political Parties* (London: Jarrold and Sons, 1916).

27. Gertrude Ezorsky, *Racism and Justice* (Ithaca, N.Y.: Cornell University Press, 1991).

28. Roger Wilkins, "The Case for Affirmative Action: Racism Has Its Privileges," *The Nation*, 27 March 1995, 409–416.

29. Stanley Fish, *There's No Such Thing as Free Speech and It's a Good Thing Too* (New York: Oxford University Press, 1994), 62.

30. Derek Bell, *Faces at the Bottom of the Well* (New York: Basic Books, 1992).

31. Barbara R. Bergmann, *In Defense of Affirmative Action* (New York: Basic Books, 1996), 62–82.

32. John B. Thompson, editor's introduction to *Language and Symbolic Power*, by Pierre Bourdieu (Cambridge: Harvard University Press, 1991), 29.

33. West, *Race Matters*, 95.

34. Manning Marable, *Beyond Black and White* (New York: Verso, 1995), 82.

35. Michael Tomasky, *Left for Dead* (New York: Free Press, 1996), 162–163.

36. Max Weber, *Economy and Society*, vol. 2 (Berkeley and Los Angeles: University of California Press, 1978), 927–930.

37. Jean Gebser, *The Ever-Present Origin* (Athens: Ohio University Press, 1985), 6–7.

38. Julia Kristeva, *Revolution in Poetic Language* (New York: Columbia University Press, 1984).

39. Roland Barthes, *The Grain of the Voice* (New York: Hilland Wang, 1985), 134.

40. Albert Camus, *The Rebel* (New York: Knopf, 1956), 296.

Chapter 7

Symbolic Violence and Social Control

DEMOCRACY AND ORDER

Democracy is thought to pose problems related to social control. In fact, in some ways these ideas are antithetical. Implied by control, for example, are differences in power; as Weber notes, someone has the ability to make others alter their behavior.[1] One group of persons has the latitude to force others to engage in actions they otherwise would not perform. In Kantian language, someone is treated as merely a means to foster another's ends.

Clearly this idea is anathema to democracy. Coercion, in short, is undemocratic. A truly democratic order is supposed to be based on legitimacy—self-imposed strictures—rather than threat or intimidation. As opposed to authority, order is predicated on the rule of law. The right to govern, therefore, is disseminated throughout society and is not the sole property of one group or another. As described by Lefort, in a democracy "power stems from the people; on the other hand, it is the power of nobody."[2]

Clearly no champion of democracy, Plato argued that this form of government is inferior to aristocracy or oligarchy. In each of these alternatives to a democratic polity, "the people" are represented by another party. Somehow these select persons have insight into the will of the masses, or at least are able to direct the passion of the populace in a constructive manner. Accompanying this skill are social differentiations that are believed to be necessary for order to prevail. If the people are left to their own devices, the worst elements of society will rise to prominence, thereby resulting in corruption and moral decay.[3]

The moral poverty of the masses has been a popular theme throughout Western history. Control became a requirement for the promotion of social prosperity. Rather than the philosopher kings promoted by Plato, real kings who had a divine mandate to lead were a key feature of Medieval society. Even subsequent to the Enlightenment, which was supposed to secularize the government, the common people were still distrusted. A close association developed between the aristocracy, or at least the rich or powerful, and those who are supposed to represent the people. In this way, the options of the plebeians, nowadays referred to as "the voters," are controlled. Because of this relationship, in other words, the sovereignty attributed to the individual by Locke is supervised and tempered. In the end, even Marxists who championed the cause of the proletariat succumbed to elitism by giving primacy to party leadership.

The point is that the people have never been trusted to govern, even in societies that claim to be democratic. A more deliberative body is required to ensure the rationality and stability of the polity. For example, either the business classes or elite government representatives have been deemed necessary to lead the masses. The people are simply too impulsive to make sound decisions.

But in a real democracy more trust must be placed in the populace. Although every person does not have to be involved in every decision—a type of micromanagement that would be impossible—ideas and proposals must be able to emanate from every segment of society. As Karl Mannheim argues, real democracy rests on the thorough democratization of culture.[4] Enough confidence must be placed in the masses to allow the free flow of information and criticism. If limits are imposed a priori on this activity, either directly through intervention or indirectly through logistical requirements, democracy is abridged.

If powerful interests overtly intervene in the process of governance to shape policies, most persons recognize that democracy is in jeopardy. Requiring candidates to be wealthy to run for office or have their ideas disseminated is a less obvious but equally effective means of control. Those who are powerful and own most of the money, for example, will certainly not fund a candidate or support legislation or ideas that threaten their social position. In both cases, unfettered influence is denied to the masses because ideas are censored before any discussion or deliberation is inaugurated.

For quite some time, direct manipulation of a democratic government has been treated as unlawful and discouraged. In this regard, attempts have been made to dismantle monopolies and other concentrations of power. On the other hand, more indirect means of control are also under attack. The influence of money on campaigns, in the form of lobbyists and other well-connected contributors, is also under scrutiny. Persons on both the Left and the Right, therefore, are pressing the issue of campaign financing reform and other measures intended to restrict the impact the unequal distribution of wealth has on the operation of government.

In general, the public is becoming restive and wary of attempts to curtail democracy. By taking this stand, the masses are demanding the authority they have never been accorded. They are asserting their right to be heard without having their wishes transmitted, and often altered, by elites who dominate economic and cultural affairs. This is not to say the masses have been radicalized, but that they have come to recognize that access to government is monopolized by various special interest groups. In this sense, the overthrow of this political status quo is unlikely.

With regard to current calls for improved democracy, the exercise of power is not being questioned, but merely the underhanded manner of this activity. Almost every politician and public official seems to be involved in a scandal. Therefore, the public has begun to set a high priority on cleaning up politics; eliminating bias and unethical schemes is on almost everyone's agenda. Being on the lookout for corrupting influences has become a public virtue.

As a result of the attention that has been directed to corruption, manipulation has become more sophisticated and increasingly distanced from traditional sources of influence. Taking their cue from the public, those in power have tried to make control appear to be in the interest of the common good.[5] As opposed to the use of force, which has a definite location, direction, and impact zone, this new form of control is imposed without appearing to be biased. Any differences in power that may exist are, for example, identified as strengthening the polity. The exercise of power is thus not necessarily bad, but only an unscrupulous or biased demonstration of this force.

THE DISAPPEARANCE OF POWER?

Having power particularized in this way in democracy, writes Lefort, often results in a reaction worse than hate: namely, contempt.[6] His point is that people feel betrayed when one group is given an unfair advantage over others. In a democracy, no one should have his or her rights usurped by another's power; no one's rights should be ancillary to anyone else's. Mass opinion—or, more accurately, a conflict of opinions—must be encouraged or dissatisfaction with a democratic polity will rapidly emerge. In the absence of this type of open discussion, persons will likely become apathetic and withdraw from public affairs. A truly civil society will cease to exist; persons will interact mostly for personal gain. Sacrificing for the people, in short, will seem to be irrational and a fruitless course of action.

During the past fifteen years, class distinctions have been rationalized by making reference to the market. Most persons tend to believe that this neutral arbiter is the most efficient means for sorting issues and ideas. According to this logic, persons are not judged by anything other than their performance. The market, writes Fromm, is driven by "abstract and impersonal demand."[7] Because of this almost infallible rationale, profitable ideas survive and others disappear; in this sense, democracy is guided by the wisdom instilled by the marketplace.

As suggested by Adam Smith, the market transcends social and cultural differences.[8] Simply stated, the market is impersonal. Persons are free at the marketplace. Any social differences that result from market performance, therefore, are real. No spurious causes are operative. If blacks, for example, happen to gravitate disproportionately to the lower end of the social hierarchy, everyone is assured that this position has been earned. No attention is paid to skin color at the marketplace, but only to performance. The market, as the saying goes, is color-blind.

Furthermore, everyone benefits from the sorting process undertaken by the market. Based on a variant of social Darwinism, the most talented people are thought to thrive at the marketplace, and once they emerge successfully from this competition, these persons begin to fill the most important jobs. The entire society benefits from these assignments because significant tasks are allotted to only the most worthy candidates. Efficiency and effectiveness of the overall social system are thus increased.

Throughout this competition, however, power is seldom mentioned. The fittest survive according to this scenario, rather than those who are the most ruthless or cunning. Even when attention is given to competition under monopolistic conditions, this situation is viewed as aberrant. According to the traditional bromide, all efficient markets eventually clear; those who avoid competition, in other words, become lazy and fat and eventually fail. In a sense, monopoly leads to its own demise.

No wonder intervention into the market is eschewed. Any interference creates disturbances that are unproductive mostly as a result of keeping unpopular ideas and unfit competitors alive. If left alone, the market will insure that society improves. The market will reward anyone who advances society, while those who do not fulfill the needs of the social system will not be enriched.

Nonetheless, this ideology of the market has not been believed by everyone. Some critics, in fact, argue that this explanation of stratification is naïve. Factors abound at the marketplace, they claim, that give an unfair advantage to specific persons or groups. In order for the market to operate effectively and justly, the state must intervene to create a level playing field.

Even in this case, however, the image must be created that intervention does not favor anyone. Everyone must be understood to benefit from government involvement in the marketplace. A classic example of this strategy is William Julius Wilson's discussion of aid to blacks.[9] Despite obvious past discrimination and lingering racism, targeting blacks for affirmative action is identified as a divisive and faulty policy. The argument is that this policy will cause animosity among whites and be resisted unless they are made to believe they also benefit from antipoverty programs. Moving toward what he calls "universal programs of reform" should be given a high priority.[10] But this alleged neutrality, claim postmodernists, represents a position that protects hierarchy and allows those with power to operate unchecked. As in all cases, this attempt at neutrality represents a chimera that benefits someone or supports some outlook.

There is no doubt that poor whites have also experienced discrimination and deserve assistance, but if the issue is eliminating poverty, the basic social and economic structure of the United States might have to be altered. Clearly, such a massive intervention is not what the conservative proponents of Wilson's recommendation have in mind. What they want, instead, is to appear even-handed. "Race-neutral" is the term preferred by conservatives.[11] No particular group is the focus of attention, but rather the improvement of everyone. Implied is that by tinkering at the margins of society, the entire system is made more efficient. Most important is that value-neutrality or color-blindness—the key components of the American creed—be reinstituted.

This facade of fairness is invoked even when vast amounts of money are given to the rich through so-called tax incentives, such as repealing or lowering capital gains taxes. Although these policies clearly benefit those who are already wealthy, the public is also thought to be enhanced. As a result of a "trickle-down" phenomenon, jobs are assumed to be generated for the working class and poor. Here again, a hidden and unbiased mechanism transforms a very focused intervention into a practice that improves the commonweal. Giving direct aid to minorities who have experienced discrimination, however, is not assumed to benefit anyone, even them. In fact, targeting assistance in this way is thought to cause discord in society; the social fabric is rapidly corrupted by this act of charity.

The rhetoric of the market, along with the weak palliatives that have become popular, is quite seductive. Persons are easily convinced that profound changes are not needed to correct any social problems that may exist. Indeed, prolonged interference will make matters worse; at most, all that is required for the social system to work effectively are minor adjustments.

Because of this inactivity on the part of the masses, those who have power are able to impose their will unmolested. After all, their interests simply epitomize what everyone desires. Consistent with the American philosophy of business, what is good for the rich and powerful is good for everyone. Why should their motives be considered suspect? They have the same interests as the rest of the people, and through their triumphs the entire polity gains stature. Those who succeed embody the so-called American Dream.

Pierre Bourdieu refers to this type of thinking as "misrecognition."[12] What he means by this term is that persons are led to deny, through the application of masterful rhetoric, events that seem obvious. Policies that benefit mostly the rich, for example, are embraced as uplifting the entire society. That such a consequence may be indirect and minimal is not treated as especially important. Most relevant is the assumption the social system will not self-destruct. In other words, the market will not respond favorably to the influence of power and violate the laws of nature. Hence, discrimination such as racism is viewed to be a momentary aberration, a faulty market strategy that will quickly backfire. This faith overpowers the logic that those who are rich will pursue their own interests first, and if profit can be made from the public they will be concerned with this domain later. Likewise, racism is treated as not benefitting anyone and unlikely to appear at the marketplace.

FAUX SELF-CONTROL

There is no doubt that certainty and security result from linking the fate of society to an infallible mechanism such as the market. Any problems that might arise will gradually disappear without much fuss. Most often, the laws of nature are followed and any societal imbalance is only temporary. Because no particular group or persons is the cause of disruption, substantial interventions are unnecessary. At this juncture, the admonishment "Don't worry, be happy" seems apropos.

Attributing regulation to unseen mechanisms, however, creates a false sense of security. Rather than internalized, control of social life has been relinquished. When people turn their interests over to market forces, they ignore the actual factors that are shaping their future. As Marx pointed out some time ago, the market consists of relationships as opposed to inanimate forces. His point is that most of the citizenry, who are not capitalists, will not control their destiny until they view themselves to be capable of creating history, particularly a society devoid of exploitation. Embracing external control devices, even those that appear to represent everyone, is inconsistent with this goal.

To borrow from Sartre, both the market and the limited correctives prescribed by liberals are based on "bad faith."[13] In other words, human *praxis* is denied to have any influence in securing order; order is attributed to factors that appear to be severed from actual behavior. Specifically, the market is imagined to have the almost magical power to reconcile all social differences with no one receiving any special treatment. Most important is that throughout this process real persons are described as if they are irrelevant. The source of security is presumed to be this regulatory device instead of the ability of persons to create a mutually satisfying environment.

In this regard, persons are attempting to "flee from what they cannot flee, to flee from what they are."[14] They are, in other words, exhibiting bad faith. Instead of self-control, they are engaged in self-negation. They refuse to acknowledge that the marketplace is comprised of people who possess different levels of status and power, and that their interaction is replete with conflict. Correcting this situation, moreover, requires far more than investing faith in the vagaries of the market. Real security is more socially grounded.

But basing security on trust and dialogue requires that manipulation be abandoned. For this change to occur, however, power differentials will have to be addressed and reduced. Although this shift in direction sounds reasonable, can elites be expected to willingly abandon their advantages? Considering the history of liberation struggles, an optimistic answer to this query is certainly naïve. Nonetheless, dialogue requires the kind of equality that is neither part of the market or liberal aid programs. Because the exercise of power is overlooked, this coercion can be expected to be manifested in new forms.

SYMBOLIC VIOLENCE

In the current noninterventionist atmosphere, the newest mode of social control is "symbolic violence." This method is extremely formalized and represents a variant of institutionalized control. In this strategy the aim is to neutralize discrimination more than ever before. "Dominant signifiers," as Guattari calls them, are attached to markers that are touted to be completely apolitical, thereby making the identification of inferiority appear to be solely in the public interest.[15] The illusion is created that nobody but society in general benefits from locating and controlling those who fail to assimilate.

In comparison to symbolic violence, institutional discrimination is crude. No matter how bureaucratized an organization may become, people are still involved. They complain and exhibit tendencies that may be considered unreliable. And through the process of selecting employees, an institution may gain the reputation of having a political orientation. Many government agencies in the United States, for example, are identified as controlled by either the Right or the Left. As a result, the public has begun to distrust these organizations. Everyone is suspicious of one agency or another.

To avoid tainting authority in this way, symbolic control operates within a space that is allegedly pristine. As described by Bourdieu, "symbolic violence . . . is violence exercised . . . in formal terms."[16] "Formal" in this context, as he goes on to add, means that the "force of the universal" is linked to the "force of the official." In the end, an apparently neutral means is available to justify norms and enforce order. Using Heideggerian terms, Bourdieu describes this process by stating that "the particular *Dasein* in its everydayness is *disburdened* by the 'they.'"[17] This "they" is the ominous force that demands assimilation; human existence (*Dasein*) is subsumed by a general sense of normativeness. Because these exalted values transcend the realm of the mundane, persons must strive to internalize these ideals. For this reason, Bourdieu declares that persons become accomplices in their repression because of symbolic violence. In other words, they regularly seek to be "normalized."

How does this process of inferiorization and redemption occur? Recalling Plato's theory of the Forms, symbolic violence is predicated on the existence of ideal norms.[18] Specifically important, persons partake of these ideals in varying degrees. Some individuals or groups reflect these standards more fully than others. Therefore, a hierarchy can be advanced that does not appear to be arbitrary. Inferiority is not a matter of opinion, but is a determination based on how closely these ideals have been introjected.

Thus far the logic of symbolic violence is clear, but how are these ethereal standards established? How are these norms unveiled so that they do not appear to be politically motivated? Here again, the dualism that plagues Western philosophy becomes relevant.

Vital to symbolic violence, writes Bourdieu, is that a special language is able to "mask the primitive experiences of the social world."[19] Based on the assumption that *doxa* can be severed from true knowledge, a unique linguistic form that is thought to be immune to the exigencies of experience is identified. The descriptions that are produced, accordingly, are touted to be facsimiles of this unadulterated reality. In Platonic terms, these linguistic practices participate in and convey these idealized standards. A specific approach to idealization, in other words, is able to masquerade as autonomous.

An important attribute of symbolic violence circumvents the problems usually associated with constraint.[20] Specifically, persons regularly volunteer to be controlled in this manner; any other response to these standards is considered to be unreasonable. Because these norms are ideal and considered to be indicative of perfection, conforming to them is believed to be logical. Transforming the body, for example, through surgery or other means is rational and thus should be pursued at every opportunity. Persons do not feel coerced to change, but instead are grateful if the alterations they choose to make are successful. Movie stars and high-paid fashion models exemplify the criteria that everyone should strive to emulate. Rather than shameful, trying to resemble these celebrities is considered to be liberating.

As noted in Chapter 3, many minority groups have succumbed to this violence. They have tried to hide their ethnic heritage by altering their appearance and rejecting native languages and customs. After all, approximating a European identity is presumed to have many rewards, including social acceptance and financial success. Contrary to what might be expected, these changes are still being made, even after the cultural liberation movements of the 1960s which tried to instill a sense of ethnic pride in persons. To many minorities, making these adjustments remains an investment in a bright future that is made with minimal regret. In the long run, however, the alienation that is often incurred may be devastating.

Because of this kind of self-denial, ethnic communities may dissolve, thereby leaving their former members with an extreme sense of loss. Specifically, language skills and cultural practices may atrophy. In the end, the cost of assimilation may be very high: A substantial identity is replaced by one that is superficial. Any success that may be realized in the mainstream does not compensate for the emptiness that is experienced.

In this regard, assimilation results in a strange hybrid. Persons are created who have undesirable traits but long to belong to the superior group; persons who renounce their heritage are allowed to mill around the periphery of society. And if enough pressure is exerted by these persons or their advocates, some mobility may be experienced by those who strive to assimilate. Always operating, however, is the proviso that rejection is possible and entirely justified. Clearly, faux integration is all that is possible when persons beg for their rights by trying to appease those who demand that everyone internalize particular cultural ideals.

Because the signifiers associated with symbolic violence are ideal rather than overtly repressive, the exercise of power does not appear to be a cause of this adaptation. In this type of manipulation, no one appears to be actually confronting minorities and making them relent. As Dreyfus and Rabinow describe, there is no ban on behavior, restriction on movement, or other evidence of the misuse of power.[21] The presence of such force would be counterproductive; overt displays of power could arouse the ire of the public due to the pretense of pluralism found in most democracies. In the case of symbolic violence, on the other hand, symbols that are ostensibly nonpartisan inscribe norms that rational persons uniformly accept. Becoming normal, however, requires a sacrifice not everyone is required to endure. Some identities are naturally acceptable, in short, while others must be jettisoned; some cultural standards are left intact and provide the model for assimilation. What should be noted is that this differentiation is not considered to be sustained by the imposition of symbols, but through the recognition that certain criteria are fundamental to distinguishing persons and cultures.[22] Symbolic violence is rational.

According to postmodernists, the Platonic stature of this evaluative scheme is an illusion. Because of the pervasiveness of interpretation, only putative idealities exist. Spivak calls these referents "impure idealization[s]," which she also recognizes to be a contradiction in terms.[23] Without iteration, she notes correctly, an ideal form cannot be supported. Without a source of commitment, in other words, norms will fade. Consequently, the pertinent question is: Who has created these standards and what practical purpose do they serve? Because these norms are interpretive and not necessarily universal, discovering who may benefit from their enforcement is crucial. This issue is especially germane in a democracy, where particularities are not supposed to be enforced as generalities. No particular position is automatically supposed to carry this much weight. This "despotism of the signifier" is unacceptable in a democratic polity, because norms are expanded in a manner that eviscerates some groups or persons.[24]

BIO AND OTHER FORMS OF ANTI-POLITICS

Several recent trends—related to the use of science-based diagnoses, computerized clinical assessments, and genes to explain behavior—have clearly illustrated the implementation of symbolic violence. The first to be discussed is the invention of elaborate classification schemes to make psychiatric diagnoses scientific. As documented by Foucault, through the development of an increasingly refined nomenclature and nosology such as the DSM series, reliable evidence is available for use in classifying patients. He facetiously refers to each of these diagnostic methods as constituting a "mathesis of light" because it allegedly introduces clarity into the uncharted realm of madness.[25]

Clinical judgments, therefore, can be rational because they are divorced from the usual fears and prejudices about the insane. Any negative labeling that might result from a diagnosis, therefore, is coincidental and unrelated to the personal or cultural features of a patient.

This conclusion is based on the premise that science is value-free and unrelated to class or cultural biases. Yet the members of the so-called "anti-psychiatry" movement challenged this belief and illustrated the political nature of diagnoses, even those that are ostensibly scientific.[26] Because of insensitivity to cultural, racial, and gender issues, for example, many diagnoses are irrelevant and harmful. The newly acquired scientific status of clinicians has transformed them into experts who render judgments based on standards assumed to have widespread validity. Armed with their scientific inventories and mounds of objective data, they have become the new control agents in various institutions, such as schools. Once a diagnosis is applied to a disruptive student who may be merely creative or bored, the academic or employment career of this individual may be ruined.

As part of this scientific arrogance, many minorities and poor persons have been diagnosed and marginalized. Following the anti-psychiatry rebellion, distrust of scientific diagnoses began to spread. A break was announced from "biological determinism and [the] positivistic category of psychoanalysis" and any other theory that denies the existential status of the patient.[27] Accordingly, exposés of the atrocities in mental institutions became popular, as witnessed by the commercial and critical success of the movie *One Flew Over the Cuckoo's Nest*. In academic circles, the passage of the new Community Mental Health Act in 1963 was applauded and gradually moved to the center of discussions about sanity. The former consensus about the benefits of scientific diagnoses and interventions shifted; these judgments and actions were no longer considered to be innocent. In fact, writes Guattari, a relationship was thought to have been discovered by advocates of anti-psychiatry "between psychiatric repression and other forms of repression."[28] In other words, psychiatry was shown to be an important mechanism of social control.

Recent advances in computer science, however, have reinvigorated those who still believe that disinterested judgments can be made about persons. Because the so-called human element is still involved in making scientifically inspired diagnoses, errors periodically occur. As might be suspected, these mistakes are not considered to be systematic or especially damaging to any particular group of clients. Nonetheless, these random problems are annoying.

As a remedy for these glitches, many diagnostic schemes have been computerized. Through the development of expert systems, their proponents claim, the rigor of a diagnosis can be enhanced. Software is available, for example, that specifies the search strategy, the logic for making decisions, and the probability that a specific diagnosis is accurate. All of the skills possessed by expert clinicians are built into these programs, minus the opportunities for error. According to the supporters of these programs, computers never have bad days, and thus computerized diagnoses are envisioned to be thoroughly accurate and reliable.

There is no doubt that these systems are rational, but accuracy is an altogether different issue. Critics of these devices, such as Terry Winograd and Joseph Weizenbaum, contend that the knowledge base of expert systems is too brittle to handle common-sense knowledge.[29] Representatives of a growing opposition, they argue that in everyday life persons make decisions in terms of values, beliefs, and other presuppositions that cannot be easily programmed. While ignoring this information, a priori categories are introduced into expert systems to classify events and persons. As a result of this discrepancy between practical know-how and programming requirements, judgments are made that relate only haphazardly to daily existence. The failure at this juncture, according to Turkle, is in not recognizing madness to be "a kind of communication or expressive demand."[30] Unable to escape from a priori designations, a computerized therapist never enters the experiential realm of the client.

Consequently, diagnoses are generated that are minimally related to cultural considerations—for example, definitions of reason, social competence, or illness—only this time the human element appears to be completely absent. Concealed behind circuits, electric signals, and lights, irrelevant assumptions operate with impunity. Moreover, imagine the trepidation of the average parent who attempts to challenge the classification of his or her child and must confront an expert that hides within a steel case shrouded by myths. What an ominous task. Nonetheless, nowadays a second opinion is often delivered by a machine that is thought to be the paragon of rationality. Even if a clinician may sometimes falter, the same cannot be said of these virtual experts.

A growing number of critics are beginning to unmask the claims about objectivity associated with computerized classificatory schemes. Even while this task is underway, a new strategy to depoliticize judgments has been gaining recognition. This tactic is an outgrowth of what Foucault calls Western civilization's love of "bio-power."[31] While not entirely new, the aim of this method is to bury the rationale for classification deep within the body and, as he describes, attribute a pathology to a "lesion, a dysfunction, or a symptom."[32] Given the irrefutable nature of a person's physical presence, who can doubt the veracity of any judgment that reflects this brute reality? To compound matters, most persons are enamored of their bodies.

The recent turn toward genes and other physiological factors to explain everything from aggression to sanity has been receiving increased support. Of course, this maneuver is partly a result of the long-time fascination with eugenics in the United States. Nonetheless, because of technological advances, geneticists are thought to have pierced farther than ever before into the root of human existence. The so-called fundamental building blocks or alphabet of life is almost at the public's disposal. What Lyotard calls "the Great Zero," the place from which all rational explanations emanate, is just out of sight.[33]

A cure or remedy for almost every ailment is claimed to be on the horizon, despite the very limited success in locating the genetic causes of maladies.

As discussed in Chapter 4, genetic arguments have become *de rigueur* in race relations. Although the focus has been on I.Q. and possibly motivation, a wider message is becoming clear. The visible disparity between most minorities and whites is unrelated to culture, environment, discrimination, or any other social variables. The explanation for this gap is found deeply imbedded within the body, and there is nothing ambiguous about physiology. Body parts are either functional or they are not. Applying this logic, the cause of racial inferiority should be easy to detect. By simply looking within a person's gene pool, the causes of all behavior will be found.

According to the advocates of this explanation, physiology is not political. What lucid person is going to argue that a particular body part is not obvious and does not have a specific purpose? But according to postmodernists, isolating genetic causes is not this straightforward. First, a genetic marker must be translated into a social behavior. Often this interpretive element is overlooked in discussions of genetics, because genes are assumed to be naturally linked to demeanor. Nonetheless, aggression is not a physiological state, but a characteristic of interpersonal relationships. Second, a social action is not simply a set of empirical properties; an interpretive context must be provided that gives particular behaviors meaning. Because of these caveats, the human element becomes a vital part of genetic explanations. Bodily signs, like all others, are not obvious but must be interpreted. Even the body is not a literal presence.[34] Given this opacity, the factor is revealed that joins politics to genetics; as mentioned earlier, the will to meaning is present that gives even genetic analysis an orientation. The human factor that is supposed to be denied is still ubiquitous and serves to make sense of all so-called objective assessments.

In each of these three examples, a similar theme is obvious. As noticed by Bourdieu, the attempt is made to link a classificatory scheme to a descriptive language that appears to be pure.[35] Science, computers, and finally, genes are thought to provide the apodictic framework required for judgments to be treated as apolitical. In the end, each of these schemes fails to be autonomous. At least initially, however, the requisite conditions for symbolic violence are met: A unique language is used that has the stature to overwhelm quotidian affairs. And, consistent with this kind of violence, designations do not appear to be imposed that represent a single perspective. The resulting classifications, however, are exact but intrusive. Despite all the claims to the contrary, bias is present in these schemes.

STEALTH CONTROL

Foucault argues that power has crept into the capillaries of existence, and that persons are currently living in the era of micropolitics. Power is not perceived to be an external force which imposes restrictions and requires personal sacrifice. Still, the same constituencies that benefit from coercive power support symbolic violence. Under what Foucault calls the "ruse of reason," symbolic violence is considered to be indispensable for maintaining traditions, classes, and other aspects of social existence.[36] Particularly in modern democracies, any other mode of control appears to be capricious.

Only as a last resort are overt displays of power exhibited in the modern world; a new modus operandi is proposed to encourage social control. The idea is that everything, including persons, is subject to similar laws. As is discussed in the previous section, these rules are made to appear to be universal; they infiltrate every fiber of existence. Acknowledging this source of reason is not repressive, for repression is negative and dictates limits. Symbolic violence, on the other hand, is portrayed to be the rational management of behavior rather than the imposition of norms.

Power is thus omnipresent. What Foucault means by this claim is not that everything has been successfully controlled, but that control "comes from everywhere."[37] As part of nature and even the larger universe, humans are expected to exhibit behavior that does not disrupt these realms. Becoming normal, accordingly, is determined by criteria to which everything and everyone should adhere. Conformity, therefore, is prescribed by a person's nature, as opposed to arbitrary standards. Normalcy is simply a by-product of maintaining a proper natural equilibrium.

Controlling persons is thus an investment in better health or a happier life. Control is now an expression of "self-affirmation," declares Foucault.[38] Clearly, science, the exercise industry, and health care organizations play a role in this charade. Nonetheless, once these normative ideals are successfully marketed, their adoption is almost a fait accompli. After all, ideals are very compelling. Those who may gain from this conformity are not perceived to be manipulative, but are often viewed as interested or even helpful. Assisting persons to get in touch with their true nature, and thereby achieving peace with the world, is recognized nowadays to be a sign of sincerity.

This approach is adopted by Charles Murray and Dinesh D'Souza to help blacks obtain jobs.[39] In order to impress an employer, their advice is that black youth should abandon the "ghetto culture." Their message is that this model of behavior is unnatural and thus frightens whites. Issuing this demand is not racist, however, because their intent is reasonable and admirable. All Murray and D'Souza desire is that black youth receive proper training and gain respectable employment. Yet despite all this evidence of concern and good will, someone retains the latitude to specify who is deemed most acceptable to work; someone can deny a livelihood to others who do not conform to arbitrary norms. This exercise of power has been obscured because of the emphasis they have placed on speech, clothing, and hairstyle. As opposed to promoting cultural inferiorization, Murray and D'Souza are simply giving black youth sound advice. In order to be competitive, these young persons simply have to accept the guidance offered by white society. This is an old story that is, sadly, mostly untrue. In the case of minorities, making these changes is not a guarantee of success. Those who have the power to make these demands, in short, do not have to respond favorably to those who plead for acceptance.

When the prevailing reality is reinforced in this way, the only response available to dissidents is defiance. With the question, "Can we fight DNA?" Baudrillard puts this concept into perspective.[40] Those who are defiant are stubborn, illogical, and presumed to reject reason. Their views, accordingly, should not receive serious consideration. For example, the reality of racial hierarchies is obvious, and those who fail to accept this fact cannot be trusted. Simply put, they are not lucid. As a result, any questions that are raised or challenges that are posed to this system of discrimination are ineffectual. The experiences of dissidents are undermined; their presence is rendered suspect without overt intimidation.

Eventually, individualism comes to be equated with conformity. Likewise, freedom and repression are almost indistinguishable. At best, as Fromm points out, "freedom from" exists—an experience that is permitted when official rules are not violated.[41] This freedom only extends so far, and precludes raising issues that extend beyond this boundary. Although sometimes appealing, these renditions of individualism and freedom are antithetical to true pluralism, which assumes order is a process that expands with the appearance of new demands. Through symbolic violence the civilizing process is complete, while the question of who prescribes the focus of control is seldom seriously raised.[42] In this regard, assimilation is not only rational but a noble act. But what is required in a democracy is a much more positive conception of freedom. The freedom that is imperative, in other words, is the ability to live in the presence of difference.

CULTURE OF DEMOCRACY: EMBODIED VISIONS

In terms of maintaining democracy, a distinction must be made between two types of norms. Simply stated, norms may be either proscribed or embodied. When these rules of behavior are proscribed and legitimized by the necessary appeal to universals, freedom is truncated. The pluralism that results is restricted, because the vox populi is prevented from speaking in a variety of ways. A priori essences, institutions, or market demands, for example, are able to curtail the growth of identity or relationships to others.

When norms are embodied, on the other hand, they reflect *praxis*. In this case, freedom is not antithetical to order, but instead establishes the parameters of all rules. These norms, moreover, are local until broader acceptance is achieved. Most important about this proposition is that norms are understood to be practical and serve someone's interests; norms are thus contingent and able to be easily contested.[43] Clearly, embodied norms and institutions are central to a democracy because multiple interests can flourish without any fear of domination.

The question is how to create such a multicultural democracy. While borrowing from E. San Juan, Manning Marable describes this as a polity where the other is not "missing, absent, or [a] supplement."[44] In this multivalent situation, persons of color are not shrouded behind a veil of whiteness or European cultural mandates. Minorities are not peripheralized by an ideology that details the cause of their moral, cultural, or intellectual inferiority. Indeed, a real democracy requires that social aggregates be recognized in their own terms; no culture, by any means, should have to speak in another's voice to be allowed to fully participate in society. This demand is far more profound than wishing for the arrival of a color-blind society. Specifically, something must be done to correct the situation where race has become a liability, whereas color-blindness is anathema to such intervention.

What has been argued thus far in this book is that democracy will remain a dream until the metaphysics of domination is deposed. There are many implications of this theoretical maneuver that need to be elaborated. Most important is to illustrate that a democratic government extends from a thoroughly democratized culture. Contrary to a melting pot, a truly democratic polity encourages the development of parallel communities that are linked through respect for one another. Being the other must not be viewed as a deficit.[45] Yet insight must be provided into how this progressive social tradition, based on multicultural unity, can be inaugurated.

NOTES

1. Max Weber, *Economy and Society*, vol. 1 (Berkeley and Los Angeles: University of California Press, 1978), 53.

2. Claude Lefort, *The Political Forms of Modern Society* (Cambridge, Mass.: MIT Press, 1986), 279.

3. Plato, *The Collected Dialogues*, bk. 8, ed. Edith Hamilton and Huntington Cairns, Bollinger Series, vol. 71 (Princeton, N.J.: Princeton University Press, 1980), 553–559.

4. Karl Mannheim, "The Democratization of Culture," in *From Karl Mannheim*, ed. Kurt H. Wolff (New York: Oxford University Press, 1971), 271–346.

5. Lefort, *The Political Forms of Modern Society*, 279.

6. Ibid., 305.

7. Erich Fromm, *Man for Himself* (New York: Rinehart and Company, 1958), 68.

8. Werner Stark, *The Fundamental Forms of Social Thought* (New York: Fordham University Press, 1963), 174–175.

9. William Julius Wilson, *The Truly Disadvantaged* (Chicago: University of Chicago Press, 1987).

10. Ibid., 120, 154–155; see also Jill Quadagno, *The Color of Welfare* (New York: Oxford University Press, 1994), 118.

11. Terry Eastland, *Ending Affirmative Action* (New York: Basic Books, 1996), 157.

12. Pierre Bourdieu, *Language and Symbolic Power* (Cambridge: Harvard University Press, 1991), 153.

13. Jean-Paul Sartre, *Being and Nothingness* (New York: Philosophical Library, 1956).

14. Ibid., 70.

15. Felix Guattari, *Molecular Revolution* (Middlesex, England: Penguin, 1984), 168.

16. Pierre Bourdieu, *In Other Words* (Stanford, Calif.: Stanford University Press, 1990), 84–85.

17. Bourdieu, *Language and Symbolic Power*, 147.

18. Plato, *The Collected Dialogues*, Bk. 6, Sec. b–c.

19. Bourdieu, *Language and Symbolic Power*, 143.

20. Ibid., 51.

21. Hubert Dreyfus and Paul Rabinow, *Michel Foucault: Beyond Structuralism and Hermeneutics* (Chicago: University of Chicago Press, 1983), 129.

22. Bourdieu, *Language and Symbolic Power*, 120.

23. Gayatri Chakravorty Spivak, "Revolutions That as yet Have No Model," in *The Spivak Reader*, ed. Donna Landry and Gerald Maclean (New York: Routledge, 1996), 88.

24. Guattari, *Molecular Revolution*, 93.

25. Michel Foucault, *Madness and Civilization* (New York: Vintage Books, 1973), 109.

26. Peter Sedgwick, *Psycho Politics* (New York: Harper and Row, 1982).

27. Phil Brown, "Anti-Psychiatry: Introduction," in *Radical Psychology*, ed. Phil Brown (New York: Harper and Row, 1973), 61.

28. Guattari, *Molecular Revolution*, 46.

29. John W. Murphy and John T. Pardek, *The Computerization of Human Service Agencies* (Westport, Conn.: Auburn House, 1991), 23–28.

30. Sherry Turkle, "French Anti-Psychiatry," in *Critical Psychiatry*, ed. David Ingleby (New York: Pantheon Books, 1980), 157.

31. Michel Foucault, *The History of Sexuality*, vol. 1 (New York: Pantheon, 1978), 140–145.

32. Ibid., 44.

33. Jean-François Lyotard, *Libidinal Economy* (Bloomington: Indiana University Press, 1993), 42.

34. Jean-François Lyotard, *Driftworks* (New York: Semiotext(e), 1984), 92.

35. Bourdieu, *Language and Symbolic Power*, 48.

36. Foucault, *History of Sexuality*, 95.

37. Ibid., 93.

38. Ibid., 123.

39. Charles Murray, *Losing Ground* (New York: Basic Books, 1984), 186–191; Dinesh D'Souza, *The End of Racism* (New York: Free Press, 1995), 505–510.

40. Jean Baudrillard, *Jean Baudrillard: Selected Writings*, ed. Mark Poster (Cambridge: Polity Press, 1988), 122.

41. Fromm, *Man for Himself*, 247–248.

42. Foucault, *History of Sexuality*, 86.

43. Stanley Fish, *Doing What Comes Naturally* (Durham, N.C.: Duke University Press, 1989), 185.

44. Manning Marable, *Beyond Black and White* (New York: Verso, 1995), 185.

45. Ibid., 192.

Chapter 8

Race and Democracy

FAILURE OF POSTMODERNISM

In a 1996 book by Tomasky, the Left is blamed for the rise of conservatism during the past fifteen years.[1] Those on the Left are criticized for their arrogance, irrelevance, and general inability to confront the problems faced by ordinary people. The average citizen, therefore, has nowhere to turn but to conservatives. Given the apparent superciliousness of liberals and radicals, a large segment of the American population has been pushed to the Right. The influence of postmodernism, claims Tomasky, has played a significant role in this trend.

Tomasky argues that the public has been alienated and often offended by the relativism that seems to be an outgrowth of postmodernism.[2] To many people, this uncertainty leads to immorality and the lawlessness that plagues modern society. Compared to the ambiguity of postmodernism, the moral appeals of conservatives sound reassuring.

But equally disturbing is how attention has been directed away from the economic issues that are the bread and butter of the Left. While influenced by postmodernists, sound economic analysis and policies have been overshadowed by discussions about identity, political correctness, multiculturalism, and so forth. Tomasky's point is that these issues not only sound silly to most voters, but demonstrate insensitivity to the economic transformation that is occurring. With restructuring and downsizing happening almost daily, why should arguments over the effective use of nonsexist language be taken seriously? When faced with losing a job, focusing on the sexist connotations of using the pronoun he or she seems frivolous. Considering this dismissive posture, the Left appears to be comprised of a cultural elite.

Doubtless, Tomasky's characterization of postmodernism is myopic. As is discussed throughout this book, postmodernists neither ignore moral issues nor dismiss economics as irrelevant. What Tomasky and similar critics of postmodernism fail to recognize is how discussions of these issues are broadened by this philosophy. Economics, for example, is placed within a larger cultural context and reformulated in terms of these wider considerations. This change, in fact, avoids the determinism and reductionism that have plagued most of the discussions of economics advanced by the Left.

Tomasky's outlook, however, is typical of the Left. The assumption is that by correcting the economy the problems present in the rest of society will abate. By giving primacy to economic issues, marginalized persons and groups will be empowered. In Marxist language, changes in the economic base will be manifested in improvements in the cultural superstructure. In less esoteric terms, enhancing economic opportunity will lead to a more inclusive society.

Although this logic is straightforward, the picture that is conveyed is misleading. In short, a causal relationship does not necessarily exist between the economy and the rest of society; the link between these two elements is much more complex than is suggested by the image of causality. The logic of racism, for example, is not necessarily altered by economic incentives or market conditions. Beliefs about inferiority, and the concomitant discrimination, do not disappear simply because an economic advantage may be gained by hiring blacks or Asians. These beliefs are insensitive to the market; they are irrational, as some writers claim, and are immune to economic rationality.[3]

There is no doubt that when the economy is growing and robust, minorities may have an easier time finding jobs. But social inclusion does not necessarily follow from improved economic opportunities. Members of minority groups have always recognized this discrepancy. All sorts of discrimination continue during both good and bad economic times. Blacks are the last hired and first fired, receive lower wages than whites for similar work, and are discriminated against with respect to advancement.[4] Because of the loose association between the economy and the presence of racism, many persons on the Left believe that economic analysis has to be expanded. Additional dimensions of discrimination that persist following economic upturns must be addressed. In this way, postmodernism has gained a following on the Left and among other critics.

An improved economy is not the panacea assumed by most traditional leftists. If the larger social project is flawed, economic changes will not have widespread impact. In the case of race relations, the metaphysics of domination is unaffected by economics. The dualism that supports the categorical separation of valuable from detrimental individual or group traits does not dissolve because of economic growth. In fact, these distinctions may serve to allocate economic opportunity; with ample justification, those who are believed to be inferior may remain at or near the bottom of society. Even if some economic advancement is witnessed by minorities, they may not be deemed acceptable to live near whites.[5] Economic changes, in other words, may not affect other aspects of culture.

In many respects, postmodernists attempt to resolve what has come to be known as the "Boasian paradox."[6] Like Franz Boas, who ignored the fact that America's commitment to evolutionary theory would stifle any serious reform of race relations, many current reformers do not recognize that unless a far-reaching cultural critique is offered, the economy will continue to operate within a context that rationalizes racism. In the end, humane intentions will be thwarted by a cultural reality that appears to be intransigent. The inferiority of specific racial groups, for example, will have to be simply acknowledged. As a result, reformers will have to eventually recognize the limits of social change imposed by the economic system or similar realities.

But because neither the economy nor any other aspect of social existence is understood by postmodernists to exist *sui generis*, this conflict that is presumed to exist between ideals and reality is averted. In the postmodern view, ideals are never antithetical to reality. Because of the interpretive bases of both ideals and reality, these viewpoints represent distinct historical projects. Recognizing one or the other is a matter of choice rather than necessity. As opposed to Boas, reformers are no longer trapped by evolutionary imperatives or other examples of the metaphysics of domination that are likely to inhibit changes designed to counteract racism.

In view of this critique of postmodernism offered by Tomasky and others, a key issue must be made clear. Good intentions and sound policies are not enough to inaugurate change pertaining to racism or any other issue. Again reminiscent of Marx, at the root of racial discrimination is a specific philosophical principle, known as the metaphysics of domination, which must be attacked if any serious reexamination of this practice is to be undertaken.[7] In the absence of this radical maneuver, anti-racist strategies will likely be compromised by the need to recognize the logic of hierarchy and the inevitability of social distinctions.

This argument is slightly different from the Marxist critique of liberals. Liberals, claim Marxists, intentionally avoid attacking relations of production in capitalism. This decision is politically motivated: The social relationships inherent to capitalism are deemed legitimate. Ignoring the metaphysics of domination, on the other hand, has political implications, but is often treated to be irrelevant to social analysis. How dualism, for example, may be related directly to racism has been obscured by focusing on the psychology or structural aspects of discrimination. Nonetheless, the philosophical project of foundationalism is antithetical to eliminating racism and must be brought to the attention of progressive critics.

POSTMODERNISM AND CLASS ANALYSIS

Anyone who pays minimal attention to writers such as hooks, West, and Gilroy, for example, understands that postmodernism has been tied to class analysis. In the case of these writers, race and class are shown to be inextricably united. Other critics who have been influenced by postmodernism, such as

Deleuze, Guattari, Foucault, and Baudrillard, have spent a lot of time assessing the various dimensions of power. Clearly, the list of postmodern writers who have emphasized the relationship between race, class, and gender would be quite long.

Why, therefore, is postmodernism commonly thought to be apolitical, or at least unable to deal with the effects of class on social and cultural life? Marxists fault postmodernists for not outlining an encompassing political program with all the required predictions about material decline and revolution. Rejection of metanarratives, in fact, robs Marxists of their causal framework and teleology, and prevents postmodernists from prognosticating wildly about the future. Even Habermas fears that moral arguments about the bankruptcy of capitalism cannot be made in the absence of the truth claims allegedly abandoned by postmodernists.[8]

Liberals such as Tomasky believe that political discussions are sidetracked by postmodernism. Serious debates should focus on job creation, tax policy, economic stimulus packages, and education and training. The traditional liberal agenda should not be obscured by forays into areas that are unrelated or tangentially linked to ameliorating the differential impact of class. In other words, liberals seem to believe that too much idealism, especially the kind interjected by postmodernism, is not politically productive. In this regard, postmodernists are raising issues that cannot be handled within the traditional liberal desire to fine-tune the prevailing economic system. Postmodernists are not concerned with merely supplying minorities with the outlook and resources required for them to adjust properly to the corporate world.

On the other hand, postmodernists view typical class analysis to be too realistic. Usually, class analysis consists of focusing on economic inequalities, identifying the skewed nature of the class structure, and discussing structural barriers to advancement. Implied by this approach to social analysis is that most of the inequalities discovered are the result of the misuse of power. A more equal and fair distribution of wealth, moreover, will result from tempering the influence of class advantages. Marxists try to correct these inequities through collectivization, while liberals propose a host of government-sponsored interventions.

Postmodernists contend, however, that these observations and descriptions can easily reify the economic system. Clearly, the assumption of traditional class analysis is that social mobility is the result of unfair competition. Specific economic advantages are transferred from generation to generation, thereby making mobility extremely difficult for outsiders. Nonetheless, describing this situation does not necessarily address the metaphysics of domination, or the system of symbolism, language, knowledge, and authority that is used to rationalize the extreme differences in wealth and power present in a capitalist society. As should be noted, these are the cultural dimensions of power, which are often made to appear neutral and universal.

Ignoring this metaphysics, for example, has allowed class analysis to be used to justify discrimination, contrary to the intent of this methodology.

Because the system of privilege is not often questioned, minorities who do not advance are referred to as inadequate. The inferiorization process is not necessarily a part of class analysis, and thus failure can easily be blamed on personal or collective defects. How the motives and intentions of minorities are distorted or undermined by social scientists or media experts, for example, is regularly overlooked, because a hierarchy of knowledge and ability is assumed to exist.[9] As a result, illustrating differential rates of mobility simply legitimizes the social system; those who advance are merely better qualified than those who do not, and thus daily existence is improved by the resulting inequality. The best persons are assigned the most important jobs in society, thereby promoting the most favorable version of order. A purely materialistic analysis of class often backfires because most persons do not appreciate the arbitrary character of social hierarchies and thus their failures only reinforce the logic of these arrangements.

To challenge racism seriously, the justification for asymmetrical social relationships must be attacked. Specifically, the rationale for white supremacy, racial exploitation, unequal economic accumulation, and cultural domination (referred to by Balibar as "neo-racism") must be subverted.[10] At this juncture is where a major contribution is made by postmodernism. As opposed to the vague moral appeals about human equality made by Marxists to end economic exploitation, explicit philosophical arguments are offered that undermine the hierarchy required to support this odious activity.

Detailed analysis is provided of the foundationalism that sustains a range of discrimination, including race- and class-based domination. Exposed are the dualism and resulting essentialism that reify identity, in addition to the privileged knowledge bases that contribute to marginalizing minority groups. Attention is directed to what at first appear to be obscure philosophical principles, in order to create a more open society. The problem is that this approach is new to American politics and seems odd or, possibly, meaningless. Clearly, cultural themes are raised that appear to be impractical or outside the usual sphere of interventions. However, treating this style of politics as unnecessary or harmful is an altogether different question. Postmodernists believe they have discovered that in the absence of this sort of investigation, the social status quo is not appreciably challenged and politics proceeds as usual.

CULTURE AND DEMOCRACY

Writers as different as John Stuart Mill and Karl Mannheim argue that democracy is a cultural or, more specifically, a particular philosophical approach to government. Rather than simply a method for electing leaders, democracy is a strategy for encouraging widespread participation in public affairs.[11] As is argued toward the end of Chapter 7, democracy is actually a form of antigovernment whereby the polity is dispersed throughout society. A proper culture must be established that fosters the inclusion necessary for this dispersion to occur. This dimension of democracy has been mostly ignored by American realists, who are thoroughly enamored of the technicalities of governance.

For the most part, traditional class analysis leads to programs designed to increase the number of minority voters. Getting more minorities into visible positions in key institutions is the aim of these campaigns. The problem is that marginalization within these institutions continues to be the rule. Blacks, for example, are regularly channelled into race-coded jobs and face a "glass ceiling" similar to that for women.[12] The point is that numerical inclusion does not necessarily culminate in participation unfettered by preconceptions about the legitimate range and validity of the contributions made by minorities. Full participation, in other words, does not automatically follow from increased access to institutions.

For full democratization to succeed, philosophical impediments to broad-based participation in the polity must be examined and refuted. The culture of capitalism is in many ways antagonistic to democracy. Despite claims about capitalism representing an aristocracy based on skill and effort, the reality of capitalist society is much different from the ideal. Elitism prevails in the form of special privileges being reserved for select persons and groups. Access to capital, participation in management decisions, control over jobs and resources, and the ability to formulate economic policies, for example, are not granted to everyone. Most persons, in fact, labor on the periphery of the capitalist system and worry daily about whether they will have a job and the right to maintain their lives. The right of persons to control their existence does not necessarily pervade a capitalist society.[13]

As with racism, much of this class discrimination is predicated on foundationalist beliefs about ability, knowledge, rights, and so forth. With foundationalism intact, someone is always able to step forward and declare his or her position to be more valuable and superior to all others.[14] Certainly, capitalists have successfully made such a claim; likewise, Europeans have tried to convince everyone that cultures are arranged in a natural hierarchy.[15] Owners and workers are thus understood to be joined in an unequal alliance similar to that assumed to exist between Europeans and the rest of the world.

For democracy to exist, however, the people—that is, the *entire* people— must permeate the polity. This change in what has been meant by the phrase "the people" will not occur until the foundationalism is undermined that allows people, knowledge bases, opinions, proposals, and other important elements of the polity to be labelled a priori good or bad, worthy of serious attention, or incidental to social affairs. Until this shift occurs, the marginalization of particular groups, ideas, and practices will be taken for granted, thereby curtailing democracy. The absence of specific groups in debates or public forums, for example, can be explained as inevitable in the age of mass politics. After all, not everyone has the basic constitution required for sustained involvement in the polity.

Different rates of participation in politics may be witnessed, but establishing an a priori rationale for these differences fosters a self-fulfilling prophecy. People who have been convinced that their views will not be treated fairly may withdraw from the political process, thereby leaving barriers to full participation unscathed. Their withdrawal, accordingly, is cited as testimony to their unfitness to govern. Moreover, increased economic opportunity does not mean that minorities will be chosen to fill new jobs, or that these persons do not believe these slots are reserved for whites. Not naïvely accepting rosy economic forecasts, however, is often used as an example that minorities are unwilling to work. Contrary to what Tomasky and other economic realists seem to think, job creation does not automatically lead to employment opportunities for everyone. Essentialism, for example, has shunted many minorities into specific career paths and encouraged them to pursue very limited personal and collective goals.[16]

In the absence of foundationalism, a true culture of democracy can be launched. Openness and tolerance can be engendered that are consistent with the democratic ideal of having everyone participate in the polity. Without the aprioris supported by foundationalist arguments, persons and issues can be judged in their own terms; they can be assessed without having to conform to specific moral or historical protocols. In this regard, identity politics, multiculturalism, and the critique of science proffered by postmodernism are not frivolous, but are vital to promoting the recognition of difference that is necessary for democracy to prevail. By attacking foundationalist philosophy, postmodernists are addressing a very subtle but potent antidemocratic force.

IDENTITY POLITICS

The dictum that "personal is political" has been an outgrowth of postmodern identity politics. Critics of this trend, most notably Fredric Jameson, contend that politics has been reduced to the level of personal idiosyncrasies which are consistent with the "me generation" syndrome and the social dissolution characteristic of late capitalism.[17] In the end, anything that does not pertain to personal gain or fulfillment is treated as impractical, or possibly personally harmful, and eschewed.

This rendition of identity politics is extremely narrow and unfair. For some time, the personal has been tied to political movements and dramatic societal upheavals.[18] Those who remember the civil rights marches of the 1960s remember both blacks and whites chanting "I am somebody" or "black is beautiful." Likewise, consciousness raising played an important part in the antiapartheid struggle in South Africa, and has been important in the radical pedagogy of Paulo Freire and the *praxis* of the women's movement. In addition, Mao, among other revolutionaries, recognized the need to reshape the human image in order to institute a new society.

Significant social revolutions have been accompanied by profound personal changes. Which comes first has been a point of contention. Nonetheless, social change is incomplete without an important shift in personal vision. Walter Benjamin calls this epiphany "profane illumination."[19] Without this expansion of consciousness the tendency to repress others may not be relinquished; new leaders can easily arise who are no different from former autocrats. Specifically, potential leaders may retain foundationalist illusions about historical or personal destiny which can be easily invoked to justify draconian political measures and dogma. According to the description provided by Irigaray, one group can harbor the destructive dream of representing the whole of humanity.[20] Do not forget that colonialism was based on such a mandate.[21]

Equally important is that during repressive periods the powerless are routinely degraded. With respect to minorities, essentialism has been used to reinforce their deprived status in society, in addition to continued attempts to inferiorize these persons. Because core traits can be attributed to persons, a clear schism can be maintained between minorities and the remainder of society. Moreover, a neatly circumscribed range of inferiority can be outlined which cannot spread and infect, for example, whites. A natural propensity to laziness or intelligence can thus be linked to particular groups or persons without much difficulty. Balibar summarizes this position as follows: Humanity is "separated by *essential* differences, or become[s] self-conscious and act[s] as if they were separated by essential differences."[22] A hierarchy of persons or groups is therefore easily established.

But because of the anti-dualistic stance of postmodernism, the architecture of essentialism is dismantled. There is no place for so-called core traits to reside untainted by interpretation. Identity is implicated in symbolism and a host of cultural factors that influence how physical features are viewed, not to mention moral traits. Most important is that persons are not necessarily restricted a priori by the unflattering images imposed by supremacists; identities are contingent and subject to revision. A "counter-memory" can be developed, contend postmodernists, that gives persons a new perspective on the past and enables repressive imperatives to be rejected.[23] In addition, there is no legitimate rationale available to assert that behavioral deviations from the political status quo signal the advance of human perversion. In time, changes may prove to be good or bad based on critical reflection and collective sentiments. With the demise of foundationalism, however, the human image is not tethered to nature or tradition, and can be remade ad infinitum.

As should be recalled from earlier discussions of the other, postmodernists do not court solipsism. Nonetheless, they insist that the personal is political. For example, without the elimination of essentialism through personal examination and critique, the reinvention of society will be difficult if not impossible. Minorities will be trapped within a perverse self-image that leads to personal destruction and the suppression of ethnic communities. This is the point that was made early on by Kenneth Clark in his classic study of the effects of segregation. Furthermore, they may even begin to give credence to the propaganda of those in power—as in the case of many Asians believing the oxymoron "model minority"—and reject potential political allies to support policies that contravene their interests.[24]

Ignoring or downplaying the personal would be a mistake in politics, but opponents of postmodernism are correct to note that the personal should not be equated with the individual, for such a tendency could prove to be politically ineffective. For postmodernists, however, the personal is always interpersonal, and thus identity politics should be interpreted as an attempt to claim self-images and social roles, and thus destinies, that were formerly denied. In other words, identity politics is always a social undertaking.

PLURALISM VS. MULTICULTURALISM

Although somewhat overshadowed by assimilation, pluralism has a noteworthy place in the history of race relations in the United States. Not everyone believes that diversity is detrimental to American society. The central problem with traditional approaches to pluralism, as illustrated in Chapter 1, is that the a prioris that pervade assimilation are also present in this approach to encouraging the growth of racial and ethnic diversity. Because of their foundational nature, these guidelines transcend and direct the development of social differences.

To borrow from Louis Althusser, the result of this foundationalism has been what might be called "pluralism in dominance."[25] With regard to American pluralists, a particular culture has served as the norm around which all others are gathered. Questions begin to arise, accordingly, pertaining to how much difference can be tolerated if a society is to survive. The fear is that this base should not be obscured by difference to the extent that commonality is jeopardized.

As a result of their commitment to foundationalism, traditional pluralists are placed in an uncomfortable position. That is, recalling Omi's and Winant's charge, pluralism is tempered by the same intractable norms embraced by assimilationists. Only now adhering to these standards is not an outright rejection of difference, but represents the recognition that some norms are truly all-encompassing and reconcile all differences. Prior to reaching this conclusion, contact between different groups is encouraged to broaden people's horizons. As the end result of this process, however, reason prevails and the best mixture of cultural imperatives emerges from this interaction. The unification of all persons into a single human family is thus finally achieved.[26]

Even within pluralist circles, therefore, concern has been directed to identifying cultural universals related to language, history, and morals.[27] Multicultural perspectives, in short, should not be allowed to cloud national standards. The question that pluralists raise, which is not asked by assimilationists, is: When should the spread of difference be halted? At what point does a further increase in difference become harmful?

Despite the dominance of assimilation, pluralism has not been viewed as especially threatening. Even conservatives have not reacted to pluralism in the manner they have to multiculturalism. Perhaps this is the case because the rationale for privilege is not really challenged by typical pluralists.[28] By making the right maneuvers, those who have power can claim to best represent society as a whole. The dominant culture that is expected to arise from within pluralism, in other words, can be claimed by supremacists.

On the other hand, such acceptance has not befallen multiculturalism. This viewpoint has been treated as the scourge of modern society and a threat to civilization. In point of fact, the eventual balkanization of society has been the fate associated with the emergence of multiculturalism.

For those in power, however, their aversion to multiculturalism is justified, but not for the reasons just cited. Indeed, the social imagery advanced by postmodern supporters of multiculturalism is the antidote for balkanization; montage preserves the integrity of the whole as effectively as hierarchy. On the other hand, the antifoundationalism of multiculturalists does not allow the universals to be introduced that halt the proliferation of difference and foster cultural dominance.

Coincident with the rejection of dualism, no difference can be accorded the status of a reality *sui generis* and be automatically treated as a cultural icon. All that can exist are cultural differences; even a so-called dominant culture is merely an interpretive option. Cultural differences may come into contact and be (re)combined in any number of ways and an inviolable strategy for organizing them will never arise. Instead, through agreements and compromises, cultural spaces are being constantly redeployed. Multiculturalists, as Barbara Herrnstein Smith remarks, do not feel the need to restrict the social "we."[29] The question of who "we" are is never really settled.

Indeed, the aim of multiculturalism is to insure that this process of give and take is not supplanted by a culture that curtails the growth of difference. In this way, true pluralism can be engendered so that societies based on difference are possible. If the goal of American society is to achieve democracy, multiculturalism is vital to the success of this endeavor, for as long as truncated pluralism is accepted, the justification for dominance remains intact. While this condition exists, the continuation of marginalization is likely.

Multiculturalism is the hallmark of a truly participatory society. Because nothing is present but difference, full social participation is encouraged; the universals that have been traditionally allowed to overwhelm difference are unavailable. Cultural difference can thus emerge unfettered and be contrasted with other differences so that each one is recognized. The universals that haunt traditional pluralism cannot legitimately arise to interfere with the arrival of new cultures and the range of interaction that is possible among them.

ESOTERIC EPISTEMOLOGICAL CONCERNS

Perhaps the most rarefied aspect of politics today, especially race relations, is the critique of science postmodernists have made an integral part of their political analysis. Veteran readers of political philosophy, however, will recognize that this gambit is not new. The members of the Frankfurt School, the Arguments and Praxis Groups, and many phenomenologists have taken a similar tack. In each case, the point has been to illustrate that the alleged value-neutrality of science is problematic.

Similar to many modern conservative, liberal, and even some radical critics, old-line Marxists wonder about the wisdom of this tactic and the intent of the members of the New Left and their mentors. After all, the strength of Marxism is its ability to make dire scientific predictions about the downfall of capitalism. Many commentators are also skeptical about Husserl's, and later Heidegger's, claim that the shortcomings of science are basically philosophical: What does philosophy, declare their critics, have to do with the alienating effects of science and technology? Proponents of science, for example, have faith that any unanticipated problems can be corrected through future technical developments. In short, science is assumed to be self-correcting.

In fact, those who have adopted this critical stance on science are often referred to as neo-Luddites. What do philosophers know about the practice and implementation of science? Those in the mainstream media and academia scoff at their claims and taunt them to abandon their television sets and refrigerators.

A similar reaction has been witnessed to the postmodern critique of science. Relativism, anarchy, and the demise of truth are thought to be the result of this ill-conceived undertaking. Accordingly, what contribution could possibly be made to politics by attacking science in this way? How are analysis and planning enhanced by excoriating what has been believed, at least since the Enlightenment, to be the most reliable arbiter of any controversy?

What these pundits are missing is an important point made both by the New Left and postmodernists. That is, science is not a value-free and neutral judge of truth. As argued in Chapter 4, science is political, or based on assumptions that are concealed by the facade of impartiality created by technique. Moreover, this illusion of objectivity has been transferred into politics, by those who have enough power to do so, to substantiate policy decisions that often discriminate on the basis of class, race, gender, and so forth. The alleged neutrality of science has allowed discriminatory practices to be instituted without drawing immediate attention to the beneficiaries of these acts. The initial defense against this criticism has simply been that everyone benefits from the exercise of science; science is neither male nor female, neither black nor white.

Postmodernists do not want science to be abandoned, or the material advances that are made possible by science halted. Instead, they are arguing that science represents a particular outlook on knowledge, which has gained legitimacy because of the widespread social acceptance of certain assumptions. The legitimacy of science, therefore, is not derived from the use of a specific methodology, but from the consensus that has been reached pertaining to the usefulness of scientific methods. Mediating science is the human element that attaches value to specific procedures and outcomes; science, therefore, does not represent an entity that has universal legitimacy or applicability.

Considering the importance of participation for the success of democracy, postmodernists recognize this shift in orientation to be very important. In short, those who are linked directly to science or can claim to have access to scientifically generated data do not any longer have the legitimacy to automatically dominate political discussions. Science is deprived of the power that has enabled it to shape debates in this way. Tied to values, the knowledge base of science is not qualitatively different from any other.

Likewise, a broader message of this critique is that legitimacy accrues from discussion, rather than form the adoption of particular techniques, methods, or apparatuses. As a result of the ability of persons to convince others through an appealing argument, legitimacy is granted to a position. With rhetoric at the root of the validity of a scientific or political program, the human element is elevated in importance.[30] Human decision making is no longer in the shadow of technique; what was thought to be a source of interpretation and error is integral to science.

Postmodernists argue that this critique of science makes possible the type of discussion that is befitting of a true democracy. No one is able to monopolize a priori the public domain; all positions have an equal status until every argument is completed. All knowledge bases, ideas, and origins of information begin as equal and are distinguished from one another as discussions proceed. The point at this juncture is not that discussants are initially neutral and objective facts should gradually dictate conclusions, but that a natural hierarchy of knowledge bases is fictitious. The fate of a knowledge claim, including those based on science, is not predetermined. A real melange of participants and contributions is thus possible, along with a montage of conclusions. There is no need, in other words, for inputs or findings to converge around a particular standard for rational conclusions to be reached. Competing truths are no longer anathema to rationality. Rather than ancillary to politics, this critique of science and similarly exalted knowledge bases is key to fostering the multivalent society extolled by advocates of democracy.

What postmodernists support is similar to what Benjamin Barber refers to as "strong democracy."[31] Postmodernists agree with his critics, however, that inclusion is not sufficient to improve democracy. The postmodern contribution is that inclusion must count; difference is irrelevant if novelty is dismissed a priori as disruptive or unproductive. Including blacks or other minorities who are identified to be irrational, unintelligent, or immoral, for example, does nothing to further democracy. The full discussion Barber wants to engender in the polity will come to fruition only when inclusion is not restricted by unchallenged foundationalist claims.

THE CULTURALIZATION OF THE "COLOR LINE"

Postmodernists have been chastised for drawing attention to what Du Bois called the "color line," the fault that has served to divide America.[32] Emphasizing race, claim most liberals and conservatives, is the wrong approach to curing America's racial ills. What mainstream society desires is a racial policy that is color-blind; developing color-blind institutions is thought to be the best approach to securing justice and democracy. Focusing on race, according to this argument, will only create hard feelings and divisiveness.

But as Cornel West documents amply, race matters in society.[33] Echoing Du Bois's claim, the color line seems to be a crucial obstacle to the promotion of democracy. While appreciably eroding civil rights, America seems to have evolved into two unequal societies—one black and one white.[34] Any move toward color-blindness, accordingly, represents an abdication of responsibility for an unsavory situation that must be corrected. Moreover, postmodernists contend that such irresponsibility casts doubt on America's claim to be concerned about the fate of democracy.

But what is accomplished by illustrating the color line to be a cultural artifact, in the manner undertaken by postmodernists? Their point is to show (1) the socially constituted nature of this demarcation and (2) the undemocratic character of this construct. Crude determinism is challenged, along with the idea that complete assimilation is useful and simply a matter of time. Racial differences are acknowledged to exist, in addition to unequal treatment of the races that is obscured by talk about color-blindness. Such obfuscation is not new, but still unproductive because untenable race domination is allowed to fester.

Contrary to the objections raised by those who are calling for a post–ethnic or ethnic-free America, recognizing the existence of race does not necessarily divide society, although a concern for social justice will likely become prominent.[35] In contrast to denial, recognizing the impact of race allows the color line to be crossed. As revealed in Chapter 5, recognizing difference and the need for persons to act jointly does not necessarily encourage the onset of chaos. Any mode of identity is dependent on the recognition of difference; "we" is not neuter but requires the existence of and comparison between I and other.[36] Talk about divisiveness, therefore, may merely reflect the fear of inclusion suggested by this new social imagery; division, after all, signals both separation and unity. Calls for fairness may signal the demise of prejudice and exploitation as more equitable relationships are established, but the passing of a corrupt society does not mean that all relationships are canceled or that new and productive ones cannot be formed.

Those who seek color-blindness violate the basic requirements of democracy. They obscure the uniqueness of persons while ignoring the differences in power that often result in discrimination.[37] They hope "the people" are homogeneous and do not try to exploit or marginalize one another. Despite this optimism, America is not a self-correcting meritocracy; in fact, many interventions from the Right are necessary to create this chimera. The unequal distribution of wealth and other resources, which accrue to persons who neither work nor are talented, has had to be rationalized in many ways to be understood to support the common good. The merits of this allocation, in other words, are not obvious to everyone.

Postmodernists, on the other hand, recognize that civility does not occur naturally. There is no mechanism similar to a market that insures the rights of individuals and groups. In short, creating a democracy is hard work and does not necessarily accompany economic change, which is a key theme of this entire book. In addition, the uniqueness of persons must be protected so that the polity remains open to everyone. Addressing the social side of race is an intervention that aids in this process. Identity construction is acknowledged, while the social impediments to personal and collective development are revealed. True democracy requires this kind of openness.

NOTES

1. Michael Tomasky, *Left for Dead* (New York: Free Press, 1996).

2. Ibid., 21–22.

3. Theodor W. Adorno, Else Frenkel-Brunswick, Daniel J. Levinson, and R. Nevitt Stanford, *The Authoritarian Personality* (New York: Harper and Row, 1950).

4. Stanley Aronowitz, "Race and Racism: A Symposium," *Social Text* 42 (Spring 1995): 34–40.

5. Douglas S. Massey and Nancy A. Denton, *American Apartheid* (Cambridge: Harvard University Press, 1993).

6. Vernon Williams, *Rethinking Race* (Lexington: University Press of Kentucky, 1996), 4–36.

7. Étienne Balibar, *Masses, Classes, Ideas* (New York: Routledge, 1994), 196.

8. Jurgen Habermas, "Neoconservative Cultural Criticism in the United States and West Germany: An Intellectual Movement in Two Political Cultures," in *Habermas and Modernity*, ed. Richard Bernstein (Cambridge, Mass.: MIT Press, 1985), 78–94.

9. Monique Wittig, *The Straight Mind and Other Essays* (Boston: Beacon Press, 1992), 26.

10. Étienne Balibar, "Is There a 'Neo-Racism'?" in *Race, Nation, Class*, ed. Étienne Balibar and Immanuel Wallerstein (London: Verso, 1991), 17–28.

11. Andrew Gamble, *Hayek* (Boulder, Colo.: Westview Press, 1996), 94.

12. Edward Herman, "America the Meritocracy," *Z Magazine*, July/August 1996, 34–39.

13. Michel Wieviorka, *The Arena Of Racism* (Thousand Oaks, Calif.: Sage, 1995), 27–28.

14. Adam Shatz, "A Friendly Nod to B-52s," *The Nation*, 29 July/5 August 1996, 25–28.

15. Colette Guillaumin, *Racism, Sexism, Power, and Ideology* (London: Routledge, 1995), 106.

16. bell hooks, *Yearning* (Boston: South End Press, 1990), 28.

17. Fredric Jameson, *The Political Unconscious* (Ithaca, N.Y.: Cornell University Press, 1981), 54.

18. Maurice Friedman, *To Deny Our Nothingness* (New York: Dell, 1967); Leo Lowenthal, *Literature and the Image of Man* (New Brunswick, N.J.: Transaction Books, 1986).

19. Walter Benjamin, *Reflections* (New York: Harcourt Brace Jovanovich, 1978), 179.

20. Luce Irigaray, *I Love to You* (New York: Routledge, 1996), 40.

21. Frank Furedi, *The New Ideology of Imperialism* (London: Pluto Press, 1994), 15–33.

22. Balibar, *Masses, Classes, Ideas*, 192.

23. bell hooks, *Killing Rage* (New York: Henry Holt and Company, 1995), 45.

24. Ronald Takaki, *A Different Mirror* (Boston: Little, Brown, and Co., 1993).

25. Louis Althusser, *For Marx* (New York: Vintage Books, 1970), 206–209.

26. Chilton Williamson Jr., *The Immigration Mystique* (New York: Basic Books, 1996), 134.

27. E. D. Hirsch, *Cultural Literacy: What Every American Needs to Know* (Boston: Houghton Mifflin, 1987), 18.

28. Anne Phillips, *Democracy and Difference* (University Park: Pennsylvania State University Press, 1993), 140.

29. Barbara Herrnstein Smith, "Cult-Lit: Hirsch, Literacy, and the 'National Character,'" in *The Politics of Liberal Education*, ed. Darryl J. Gless and Barbara Herrnstein Smith (Durham, N.C.: Duke University Press, 1992), 83.

30. Stanley Fish, *Doing What Comes Naturally* (Durham, N.C.: Duke University Press, 1989), 298.

31. Benjamin Barber, *Strong Democracy: Participatory Politics for a New Age* (Berkeley and Los Angeles: University of California Press, 1984).

32. W. E. B. Du Bois, *The Souls of Black Folk* (Greenwich, Conn.: Fawcett, 1961), xiii, 138–139.

33. Cornel West, *Race Matters* (Boston: Beacon Press, 1993).

34. Andrew Hacker, *Two Nations* (New York: Macmillan, 1992).

35. David A Hollinger, *Postethnic America* (New York: Basic Books, 1995), 107.

36. Irigaray, *I Love to You*, 104.

37. Ibid., 44.

Selected Bibliography

Asante, Molefi Kete. *Kemet, Afrocentricity and Knowledge*. Trenton, N.J.: Africa World Press, 1992.

Balibar, Étienne. *Masses, Classes, Ideas*. New York: Routledge, 1994.

Barthes, Roland. *Image, Music, Text*. New York: Hill and Wang, 1977.

———. *The Grain of the Voice*. New York: Hill and Wang, 1985.

———. *Writing Degree Zero*. New York: Hill and Wang, 1968.

Buber, Martin. *I and Thou*. New York: Charles Scribner's Sons, 1970.

Derrida, Jacques. *Writing and Difference*. Chicago: University of Chicago Press, 1978.

Ezorsky, Gertrude. *Racism and Justice*. Ithaca, N.Y.: Cornell University Press, 1991.

Feyerabend, Paul. *Science in a Free Society*. London: NLB, 1978.

Fish, Stanley. *Doing What Comes Naturally*. Durham, N.C.: Duke University Press, 1989.

———. *There's No Such Thing as Free Speech and It's a Good Thing Too*. New York: Oxford University Press, 1994.

Foucault, Michel. *The Archaeology of Knowledge*. London: Routledge, 1989.

———. *The Birth of the Clinic*. New York: Vintage Books, 1975.

———. *Power/Knowledge*. New York: Pantheon, 1980.

Gilroy, Paul. *The Black Atlantic*. Cambridge: Harvard University Press, 1993.

———. *Small Acts*. London: Serpent's Tail, 1993.

———. *There Ain't No Black in the Union Jack*. London: Routledge, 1995.

Goldberg, David Theo. *Racist Culture*. Oxford: Blackwell, 1993.

Guattari, Felix. *Molecular Revolution*. Middlesex, England: Penguin, 1984.

Guillaumin, Colette. *Racism, Sexism, Power, and Ideology*. London: Routledge, 1995.

hooks, bell. *Yearning*. Boston: South End Press, 1990.

———. *Killing Rage*. New York: Henry Holt and Company, 1995.

Irigaray, Luce. *An Ethics of Sexual Difference*. Ithaca, N.Y.: Cornell University Press, 1993.

———. *I Love to You*. New York: Routledge, 1996.

Kuhn, Thomas S. *The Structure of Scientific Revolutions*. Chicago: University of Chicago Press, 1975.

Levinas, Emmanuel. *Totality and Infinity*. Pittsburgh: Duquesne University Press, 1961.

Lyotard, Jean-François. *The Postmodern Condition*. Minneapolis: University of Minnesota Press, 1984.

———. *Libidinal Economy*. Bloomington: Indiana University Press, 1993.

Marable, Manning. *Beyond Black and White*. New York: Verso, 1995.

Marcuse, Herbert. *One Dimensional Man*. Boston: Beacon Press, 1964.

Murphy, John W. *Postmodern Social Analysis and Criticism*. Westport, Conn.: Greenwood Press, 1989.

Myrdal, Gunnar. *An American Dilemma*. New York: Harper and Brothers, 1944.

Park, Robert. *Race and Culture*. Glencoe, Ill.: Free Press, 1950.

Sartre, Jean-Paul. *Anti-Semite and Jew*. New York: Schocken, 1969.

Sontag, Susan. *Against Interpretation*. New York: Farrar and Straus, 1966.

Takaki, Ronald. *A Different Mirror*. Boston: Little, Brown, and Co., 1993.

Tomasky, Michael. *Left for Dead*. New York: Free Press, 1996.

Tucker, William H. *The Science and Politics of Racial Research*. Urbana: University of Illinois Press, 1994.

West, Cornel. *Prophetic Reflections*. Monroe, Maine: Common Courage Press, 1993.

———. *Prophetic Thought in Postmodern Times*. Monroe, Maine: Common Courage Press, 1993.

———. *Race Matters*. Boston: Beacon Press, 1993.

Wittig, Monique. *The Straight Mind and Other Essays*. Boston: Beacon Press, 1992.

Index

ABOUT THE AUTHORS

JOHN W. MURPHY is Professor of Sociology at the University of Miami.

JUNG MIN CHOI is Assistant Professor of Sociology at Barry University.

Both have written extensively and are the coauthors of several books, including *The Politics and Philosophy of Political Correctness* (1992) and, with K. Callaghan, *The Politics of Culture* (1995), both published by Praeger.

ISBN 0-275-95664-4

90000>

EAN

9 780275 956646

HARDCOVER BAR CODE